The
Southern
Agrarians

PAUL K. CONKIN

THE UNIVERSITY OF TENNESSEE PRESS / KNOXVILLE

Library of Congress Cataloging-in-Publication Data

Conkin, Paul Keith.
  The Southern Agrarians / Paul K. Conkin. — 1st ed.
    p. cm.
  Bibliography: p.
  Includes index.
ISBN 0–87049–560–7 (alk. paper). ISBN 0–87049–561–5 (pbk. : alk. paper)
    1. Agrarians (Group of writers) 2. Fugitives (Group of writers)
3. American literature—Southern States—History and criticism.
4. American literature—20th century—History and criticism.
5. Authors, American—Southern States—Political and social views.
6. Authors, American—Southern States—Biography. 7. Authors,
American—20th century—Biography. 8. Southern States—Intellectual
life—1865- . 9. Literature and society—Southern States—
History—20th century. 10. Politics and literature—Southern
States—History—20th century. 11. I'll take my stand. I. Title.
PS261.C56 1988
810′ .9′975—dc19   87–22496
                                                              CIP

The Southern Agrarians

Contents

Illustrations

Preface

The Southern Agrarians are very familiar to scholars. They have received much loving attention from historians and literary critics. Biographers have revealed fascinating personalities. Critics have thoroughly evaluated their best prose and poetry. But such attention to individuals and works of art has left untold much of the story of how a varied and fascinating group of individuals interacted, how they matured their hopes and dreams, how they struggled to achieve them, and how they ultimately suffered decline and defeat. I now want to tell that story. It involved deep and abiding friendships as well as original thinking and eloquent writing.

In American letters, both the Fugitive poets and the Agrarian reformers have a very distinctive status. Their writing, in each case, matured within an intense, ongoing seminar or discussion group, and among close personal friends. The dialogue, and some personal bonds, continued for half a century. Equally distinct were the intense sectional or regional loyalties that bound together the Agrarians. Never before had so many regionally based scholars and artists worked together as a group over such a long period of time. Most American writers have acknowledged their affinities with other intellectuals, or indulged a challenging dialogue in print or at meetings, but most have largely worked alone. Even anthologies or collections have been more nearly compilations than products created out of group discussions and enduring personal friendships.

My focus is upon people and their beliefs and action. I have tried to interweave group biography and intellectual history. Given the contributions of John Crowe Ransom and Allen Tate to a type of formal, internal criticism, I feel some need to defend this focus. It is not my purpose, in this book, to evaluate the writings of the Agrarians on esthetic grounds. My subject is not works of art, but artists as moral and political activists. I am interested not in formal or rhetorical skills but in the beliefs and values reflected in works of art. My purpose is that of almost any humanistic scholarship — to force people to confront their own identity. The Agrarians forced not only southerners, but all Americans, to such introspection, to a sustained reevaluation of their beliefs and preferences. I hope their message will be clearer, and more challenging, as a result of the tale I now tell.

I should not begin that story without a brief confession. I am not a remote or detached observer of the Agrarians. The story touches upon too many aspects of my own past. I grew up on a small, in part subsistence, preelectrical Tennessee farm. I financed my college education by the returns from growing tobacco. I completed my graduate degrees at Vanderbilt in the 1950s. I took courses from Herman Clarence Nixon, an Agrarian who had fought courageously for civil rights. I met Donald Davidson, the Fugitive poet and Agrarian who was by then a determined defender of segregation. I completed a dissertation, and first book, on subsistence homesteads and back-to-the-land efforts in the New Deal. Recently, I completed a long history of Vanderbilt University. In it I included a frustratingly brief section on both the Fugitives and Agrarians, and now simply tell the fuller story that space precluded in that book. I am now a Vanderbilt professor. In all these ways, and more, the Nashville Agrarians seem almost a part of my family.

I should not end this Preface without some acknowledgments. I first tried to tell the story of Agrarianism in my earlier biography of Vanderbilt University — *Gone with the Ivy*. But space limitations allowed only a severely compressed chapter. Thus, my many debts extend back to that earlier research, and to the institutional support I received from Vanderbilt University. Once again, I want to thank

Patricia S. Miletich, who assisted me on the Vanderbilt book, and the several people in Special Collections at the Heard Library who made pleasant my archival research. I owe much to my colleagues in the Department of History, who because of this project suffered the frequent distraction of their chair, and to the Department staff—Anna Luton, Mary Frances Moore, and Sally Miller—who helped so much in the typing and preparation of the manuscript.

I.

The Fugitive Prelude

In a sense, the origins of Southern Agrarianism stretch back to about 1915. By then, a half dozen young men in Nashville, Tennessee, most either students or faculty at Vanderbilt University, began gathering periodically for some heavy philosophical discussions. After the war those few, joined by an equal number of younger men, switched their concern to poetry and for four years published a small monthly journal, *The Fugitive.* After 1925, four of these Fugitives, soon joined by friends or colleagues, turned their attention to political and economic issues, and particularly to the problems of the South. These discussions first found outlet in what became a famous book, *I'll Take My Stand,* and in a crusade called Southern Agrarianism. These two decades of intense intellectual dialogue directly involved about twenty people.

The young intellectuals who argued in Vanderbilt hallways or in Nashville homes never agreed with each other on all issues. They did share important commonalities of background—geographical origin, educational experiences, and religious heritage. Brilliant, creative, eloquent, they managed only brief and ephemeral alliances at the level of broad, general, but inherently ambiguous platforms. Only briefly, and this after 1933, did a group of Agrarians share enough in the way of common goals to make up a movement. Just as it is more accurate to refer to a remarkably similar group of young men and women a century earlier in New England as a Transcendentalist circle, so these Nashville intellectuals made up a loose circle, with vague outer boundaries and frequent shifts in membership.

Only two of the young men who joined in intense discussions before World War I became later Agrarians—Donald Davidson and John Crowe Ransom. Only two additional but younger Fugitives—Allen Tate and Robert Penn Warren—also became Agrarians, with Tate much more critically involved than Warren in both the Fugitive and Agrarian enterprises. Their involvement made up the clearest continuity between the Fugitives, an interacting and nonpolitical group of poets, and the intensely political Agrarians. The dominant leaders in each circle were the same—Davidson, Ransom, and Tate. The story of both groups is closely linked to their developing interests and concerns, to their interaction with each other, and to their indispensable intellectual leadership. Neither group would have gathered or achieved fame without the big three. And critical to the role of these three in Agrarianism was their interaction with each other as Fugitives and the enduring friendships that resulted from that interaction.

Neither the Fugitives nor Agrarians had any official tie to Vanderbilt University. To some extent, both groups suffered a degree of rejection or hostility from stuffy and unbearably conventional Vanderbilt administrators. In both the twenties and the thirties, the bulk of the University community never read or understood the Fugitive poems or sympathized with Agrarian arguments. The Fugitives attracted some favorable attention to Vanderbilt, but the Agrarians largely created an unwanted notoriety or embarrassed the University by the ensuing political and economic controversies. Only years later did official Vanderbilt claim, and then exploit, the achievements of those who ultimately provided its best claim to national recognition. Yet, most Fugitives (twelve of fifteen identified on the masthead of the small magazine) and Agrarians (ten of twelve contributors to I'll Take My Stand) were Vanderbilt professors, students, or alumni.

Despite official hostility or benign neglect, the University setting provided a necessary condition for the gathering and flowering of those two overlapping groups. The academic assets of Vanderbilt, its faculty and libraries, attracted able professors or students to

Nashville. But any university had such assets, and larger, more prestigious northern universities had a much more plenteous supply than a provincial Vanderbilt. That a few brilliant young intellectuals happened to be at Vanderbilt at the same time and that they were able to join in exciting, supportive discussions was, from the university's perspective, serendipitous. The rich intellectual harvest was in no wise contrived. Unexpected, unappreciated, and unearned, it was an academic form of unmerited grace.

But some distinctive attributes of Vanderbilt played a role in the intellectual renaissance. From 1875 to 1914, Vanderbilt remained the only university supported by the Methodist Episcopal Church, South. Despite early, and generous, support from Cornelius Vanderbilt and his descendants, and despite a brief flowering in the 1890s, Vanderbilt began the new century with major handicaps. Its endowment stagnated. Its ablest faculty left. Its student body became increasingly provincial. The Bishops of the Methodist church, although begrudging in financial support, tried in the new century to exercise an unwanted control over faculty and policies. At the same time, Vanderbilt's able chancellor, James H. Kirkland, tried to minimize the church connection, in part to attract badly needed foundation support. A clash over policies, and legal ambiguities involving the powers of the church as against the Board of Trust, led to an extended legal battle won in 1914 by Kirkland and his Board. The church, disillusioned by the outcome, dropped all ties to Vanderbilt, leaving it as an independent, ambitious, but financially strapped southern independent university.

Despite these problems, Vanderbilt remained the strongest university in the upper South. Its faculty was able enough to offer a credible M.A. in the humanities and social sciences. It provided the best educational opportunities affordable and accessible for the most academically gifted young men and, increasingly, young women in the trans-Appalachian South. For those academically gifted students in the region who could not afford to enroll in northern universities or who were fearful of the challenges in an alien North, Vanderbilt provided the best available higher education. This meant, at any one time, a pool of exceptionally able but homogeneous southern students. Vanderbilt drew the largest proportion of these students from central and western Tennessee and Kentucky, from northern Georgia, Alabama, and Mississippi, and from parts of Arkansas and Texas. Notably, with only one or two exceptions, the Fugitives and Agrarians all grew up in this region.

The College of Arts and Science at Vanderbilt, until after World War I, adhered almost rigidly to a classical curriculum. Its B.A. graduates had to complete courses in both Greek and Latin, which also remained among the requirements for admission. The typical Vanderbilt student took half his courses in English, Philosophy, and Classical and Modern Languages. In these subjects, Vanderbilt had been able to recruit professors with a national reputation and considerable scholarly achievement. One word best described the prewar Vanderbilt culture — *literate*. The ablest students became deeply involved in literary issues, joined in literary clubs, and struggled to gain a mastery of writing skills. The quality of student publications was unexcelled in any other American university.

In later reminiscences, some as late as 1956, the Fugitives with Vanderbilt degrees emphasized above all else their classical education. As they looked back, they particularly celebrated a few professors, among them some of early Vanderbilt's ablest scholars: classical scholar, later Dean, Herbert C. Tolman; a somewhat eccentric, German-trained philosopher, Herbert Sanborn; and from 1912 on, the dynamic, evangelical head of the English Department, Edwin Mims. Mims's relationship to the Fugitives and Agrarians would be complex. His large, popular courses on the romantic poets at first inspired, then often incited rebellion among his abler students. His progressive, "New South" political views horrified the later Agrarians. But Mims built a strong English department, valued creative writing as much as scholarship, and by his old-fashioned values and standards provided a foil for such rebellious students as Allen Tate. The sum of all this — Vanderbilt did offer needed scholarly resources as well as a spur of intellectual ferment to its gifted students. And in a familiar, nonalienating southern environment.

The experience of later Agrarians at Vanderbilt began in 1903, when a fifteen-year-old John Crowe Ransom matriculated. He would be the mentor of the Fugitives, the philosopher of the Agrarians. Born in Pulaski, Tennessee, he was the son of one of the most respected ministers of the Tennessee Conference, Methodist Episcopal Church, South. In fact, his paternal grandfather had also been a Methodist minister. Because of the tradition of itinerance in Methodism, bishops assigned Ransom's father to new pulpits at least every five years. His family thus moved frequently, but always in an orbit with Nashville as its center. He came from what, by current Tennessee standards, was an exceptionally talented and educated family. His father, a linguist, a college graduate, had earlier served the church as a missionary in Brazil, and was a supportive and solicitous father. Ransom's academic and literary success grew naturally out of a family environment that was refined, even aristocratic, and far removed from the competitive pressures and the pecuniary values of a business civilization, or what Ransom always rejected. Although intensely ambitious, academically competitive, Ransom always celebrated the virtues of a country gentleman, with leisure at the top.

Until ten, Ransom did not attend the poor public schools of Middle Tennessee. His parents tutored him and pushed him far ahead of boys his age. Then, after one year in a public school, he came to the academically respected Boman school in Nashville, where he completed a heavily classical high school curriculum. Despite his youth, he achieved more at Vanderbilt than any former student. Perhaps to his benefit, he had to suspend his Vanderbilt studies for two years (1905–1907), which he spent teaching in two different high schools. By graduation in 1909, he had the best academic record at Vanderbilt (Founder's Medalist in his college) and had edited both the student literary journal and newspaper as well as gaining Phi Beta Kappa. After teaching Latin and Greek for a year in a prep school, he won a coveted Rhodes scholarship.

At Oxford he spent three years in what he viewed as a difficult course of study ("The Greats"), one which utilized his exceptional training in Greek and Latin. He read mainly in philosophy and became a disciple of Aristotle and Kant. But Ransom proved anything but an academic drudge, to his later regret. Letters home show him spending half his time in travel and sports. He loved golf, tennis, chess, and card games and delighted in conversation and social intercourse. To his embarrassment, and regret, he barely failed to gain first class honors, losing on a 3–2 vote by his examiners, a failure that he could have avoided by even slightly more disciplined work. Nonetheless, his still prestigious Oxford B.A., although not

comparable to a German or American Ph.D., was the sole basis of
Ransom's later academic career. He returned to America with lofty
academic ambitions. Largely for financial reasons, he taught his
first year at the highly regarded preparatory Hotchkiss School in
Connecticut, while seeking a university job in larger northern universities. At Hotchkiss he developed an intense interest in English
literature, and, almost by default when other possibilities fell through,
accepted a lowly instructorship in English back at Vanderbilt in
September 1914. Almost immediately he joined in, to a large extent
led, the discussions that produced *The Fugitive*.[1]

Just as Ransom began his teaching at Vanderbilt, the younger (by
five years) Donald Davidson was able to get enough funds to resume his aborted undergraduate studies at Vanderbilt. Davidson
was born in 1893 at Campbellsville, Tennessee, near Ransom's birth-
place of Pulaski. The two young men shared so much as to make
them, as Davidson later put it, de facto cousins. Davidson's father
was an ill-paid public school teacher, later a county superintendent,
who moved frequently to new positions. Like Ransom, Davidson
gained his early schooling at home and at this early age began to
develop his later, at times intense, contempt for most public schools,
a distrust related to his father's frustration in Tennessee schools. He
gained both his final elementary and his secondary education at
private academies, academies that were far from elite but which
emphasized classical languages and intense self-discipline. For example, Davidson took four high school credits in Latin, three in
Greek, plus four years in English and mathematics. His mother was
a musician, and young Donald early revealed his own talent in this
area and even considered a career in music. This interest in music
he shared with both Ransom and Tate. On borrowed money, Davidson matriculated at Vanderbilt in 1909, the year Ransom graduated.
For financial reasons, he had to suspend college work after a year,
spending the next four years teaching in two private academies. He
was able to resume college at Vanderbilt in 1914 only because of
part-time teaching at a nearby academy. Despite the demands of
two jobs, he had time to join in the early Fugitive discussions and,
in fact, first invited his Shakespeare professor—Ransom—to the discussions. Davidson almost completed his B.A. in 1916, after three
years of superhuman effort. But he had to take a teaching job back

at an academy at Pulaski, where he met a young Latin teacher at Martin College, Theresa Sherrer. This abundantly talented Ohio native, an Oberlin graduate, later became his wife. In 1917 Davidson volunteered for military service and was able to use military science credits to earn his Vanderbilt B.A.[2]

Until 1914, most literary discussions at Vanderbilt took place in the Calumet Club, an honorary society made up of Vanderbilt journalists or would-be writers. This all changed because of the efforts of one Sidney Mttron Hirsch. Eccentric, independent-minded, Hirsch had not attended Vanderbilt or completed degree work at any university. His half-brother, Nathaniel Hirsch, and also a sister, took their degrees at Vanderbilt and first brought able classmates to the Hirsch home, to the delight of Sidney, who liked nothing more than presiding over brilliant conversation. The awed students included several future Fugitives: William Yandell Elliott, who later became an eminent Harvard political scientist; Alec Stevenson, son of Professor J. B. Stevenson of the Vanderbilt School of Religion, editor of the student literary journal, *The Observer,* and a later Nashville businessman; Stanley Johnson, later a disaffected instructor in the Vanderbilt English department and a novelist and free-lance writer; and Davidson, who soon brought Ransom to the good discussions and hospitality at the Hirsch home on nearby 20th Avenue. In the fall of 1915 a new Vanderbilt assistant professor, Walter Clyde Curry, began joining some of the sessions. Curry, who was to become a major Chaucer scholar, enjoyed philosophical and esthetic discussions. He completed a circle of seven young, unmarried men that continued to meet together until the disruptions of war in 1917. By their later memories, the discussions ranged far and wide but usually came to rest on deep philosophical and metaphysical issues. The two dominant figures were Hirsch and Ransom.[3]

Hirsch played an essential role in the flowering of the Fugitive group, and not just as a host. He was the cultural outsider. The young Vanderbilt men, except for Curry, were all from Nashville or the surrounding countryside, and all were native stock, evangelical Protestants. Hirsch was a nonpracticing Jew from a prominent mercantile family in Nashville. But his Jewishness scarcely accounted for his special identity. Jewish-Gentile interaction was a normal aspect of student life. Hirsch fit no labels. He was a bit of an intellectual dilettante, with his own special enthusiasms. He had had a rather strange career, one undoubtedly embellished with each fascinating recounting. A large, handsome man, he had served in the peacetime Navy, traveled in the Orient, served as an artist's model in Paris, and purportedly knew many famous people around the world. He successfully projected a worldly, cosmopolitan, sophisticated outlook to his awed guests. More significantly, he professed familiarity with ancient and hidden wisdom, Occidental and Oriental, much present in the occult meanings hidden in ordinary words. His position, drawn from Cabalist or Rosicrucian traditions, properly mystified his young guests. More recently Hirsch had dabbled in drama and the theater and in 1913 had composed and directed a spectacular Greek pageant performed in front of Nashville's replica of the Parthenon.

None of the young men fully understood Hirsch. His mind seemed undisciplined by logic, as he leaped from one topic to another or professed to derive half the secrets of the universe from a detailed etymological investigation of a single word. For Hirsch ordinary surface appearances always masked deeper truths, truths that often emerged, unrecognized, in poetry. Hirsch loved people, loved to talk, and thus flattered his guests by his attention and often by his uncritical praise. They flattered him by taking him seriously. For unsure youth just venturing into creative endeavors, Hirsch's praise provided a needed self-confidence. In some ways Hirsch was already a pathetic man, with evidence of major psychological problems. He had no real career, no direction in life, no chance of future achievements. He lacked the needed discipline. His only glorious achievements, perhaps mythical, were now all in the past. Thus he gained much from the Fugitives and took an almost parental pride in all their achievements. But, in time, the young men all outgrew Hirsch. They continued to respect him, to love him for his generosity of spirit, but they eventually came to recognize that his beguiling obscurities concealed not some deep truths but only his own confusions. Out of personal respect they never let on that they knew.[4]

Ransom was the perfect counterweight to Hirsch. When he joined the emerging discussion group he tried to discipline Hirsch's scattergun insights. No one ever succeeded in that. But the two stimulated the best in each other, even as their soaring interchanges often left the undergraduates completely mystified. Ransom had a native brilliance, as reflected in his academic successes and philosophical achievement at Oxford. He did not have the temperament or the skills of a professional philosopher. He never easily travelled back and forth between basic assumptions and working theories, but rather worked out, often with an exacting logic, the implication of his own ever-shifting intellectual commitments. In the discussions Ransom seemed unusually detached and logical, always on guard against verbal obscurities or needless flights of fancy. For the young men he was mentor and critic. Yet they did not approach him in fear and trembling. Ransom seemed so detached from the critical game, so far removed from any intellectual insecurity, any ego vulnerability, that no one saw any personal animus in his most devastating remarks. He was able, therefore, to remove from what soon became an ongoing seminar any deadly ideological explosives. Not only did he raise his comments to a seemingly impersonal and therefore nonthreatening level, but he kept pulling those of others back to the pure intellectual game. Not that Ransom was as detached as he seemed; he later suffered some bruises to his own ego. But he was able to establish game rules that allowed a dialogue to continue for years, a dialogue that placed ever heavier demands on participants, yet in an atmosphere that reinforced a growing sense of self-mastery. Discussion groups rarely achieve this for very long. They either break up or gravitate into a comfortable rut. Hirsch, half guru and half clown, always ready to find great truths in any youthful comment, provided the needed stimulus toward originality; Ransom, with his dry detachment, set the standard for rigor and for intellectual self-discipline.[5]

The prewar seminar remained, at best, a preparation for poetic creativity. The members did not meet to criticize poems, although they talked a great deal about art and esthetics. But back on campus the participants read and discussed poetry in the Calumet Club, in Edwin Mims's famous course in English literature (he required his students to memorize long sections from Browning and Tennyson), and in Ransom's course on Shakespeare. And, largely in private, they did what most college students do — they wrote verse. In 1915, according to the later memories of Donald Davidson, Ransom sheepishly approached him with a poem, inviting comments. This, surprisingly, was Ransom's first effort, at least as he understood the demands of a poem. Perhaps characteristically, Ransom made the intellectual decision to write a poem and then carefully crafted it. Composition for him involved choice and deliberation as well as the assumption of certain formal constraints. Davidson applauded the poem, and Ransom soon successfully submitted several poems for publication. Just before the war he submitted a bundle of them to a press and through the critical support of Christopher Morley and Robert Frost was able to publish the small volume in 1919 in England under the title *Poems About God*. Ransom later felt apologetic about this early effort; the poems received little critical acclaim, at least in America. Conventional in form, they were non-traditional in subject matter. In the poems Ransom aired some of the metaphysical concerns explored, and not resolved, in his discussions with Hirsch. Even this early he flirted with an unresolved dualism between heart and head, between the qualities of immediate experience and abstract reason that would help shape his later critical theory and his Agrarian essays. This early volume incited Ransom's interest in poetic theory and the writing of better poetry. It also gave him a professional reputation, a degree of eminence not enjoyed by his students or young colleagues. Had the war not intervened, the discussions at Hirsch's apartment would have turned to poetry at least by 1918.[6]

The war only postponed the next, poetic stage of the discussions. The emerging Fugitive circle led charmed lives. None died or were even wounded in the war. Ransom and Davidson both enlisted with the first officer candidates who left Nashville for Fort Oglethorpe in May of 1917. Here they met from time to time and even read each other's poems. Elliott, Stevenson, and Johnson all volunteered or were drafted. Of the group, only Hirsch and Curry remained in Nashville. Lieutenant Ransom went early to France but instead of front-line duty served in an officers' training program at Saumur. Davidson moved into combat only a few days before the armistice, taking with him a manuscript of *Poems About God*. Vanderbilt graduates, by their education eligible for officers' training, flocked to Saumur, creating there an alumni group that revolved around Ransom. Stevenson trained there as did another Vanderbilt student—William Frierson—who would briefly join the Fugitive cir-

Lieutenant Donald Davidson in World War I uniform

cle after the war. At war's end, Ransom, Elliott, Stevenson, and Frierson were able to enroll in French or Swiss universities at Army expense and in this interlude gained a direct acquaintanceship with the new schools of French poetry. In 1919 these future Fugitives slowly returned home, presumably much wiser for all their adventures. Ransom, at least, sought a northern position and did not really want to return to Vanderbilt. Earlier, in long letters to his family, he had listed the advantages of urban life as opposed to village life.[7]

Not surprisingly, the returning veterans sought out Hirsch and resumed their prewar seminar. Sidney Hirsch had meantime moved west of the campus to the Whitland Avenue home of his sister and brother-in-law, Rose and James Frank. The Franks became generous hosts to the group. James Frank, a businessman, became a member of the Fugitive circle and later contributed a few carefully crafted poems to *The Fugitive*. Sidney, bothered by a somewhat mysterious ailment, was confined to a chaise longue but from it hosted the gathering in almost regal style.

Very soon poetry dominated the resumed discussions. Ransom's absorption in the problems of poetics insured this. Hirsch welcomed the subject, one always related to the universal wisdom he espoused. The two men once again worked their magic with the growing number of newcomers. Curry, who occasionally wrote sonnets, rejoined the group but soon would be too involved in scholarship to attend all the sessions, which fell into a biweekly Saturday evening pattern. Elliott was back in graduate school; Frierson completed his senior year. In 1920 both had to leave the magical group as they moved to Oxford on Rhodes scholarships. Stevenson soon returned to Nashville because of the death of his father (he had worked for Philadelphia newspapers), and after brief assignments with the *Nashville Tennessean* and the *Nashville Banner* he went into banking and securities. Davidson, discharged in 1919, now married and in desperate financial straits, unsuccessfully sought a position at Vanderbilt but had to take a one year position at Kentucky Wesleyan College. He worked on a newspaper in the summer of 1920 and then began M.A. work at Vanderbilt in the fall, assisted by an instructorship in the English department. Stanley Johnson did not return to Nashville until 1921 to enroll for graduate work in the English depart-

James Frank, host to the Fugitives and poet

ment. Before that he had taught two years in the Philippines and written his first novel. In a later 1925 novel, *The Professor,* he satirized the Vanderbilt English department. A few other students came occasionally, including Alfred Starr, subsequently a local motion picture entrepreneur and an infrequent contributor to *The Fugitive.* Of the younger group, Davidson was most committed to a career in literature. But the others all dabbled in poetry, even though they would never become so engaged in critical theory as Ransom and Davidson.[8]

This was not true of a new member of the group. As of about 1921, Davidson invited John Orley Allen Tate, then a junior at Vanderbilt, to attend their seminar. Tate was an *enfant terrible,* a slim, wiry, intense, large-headed prodigy out of Kentucky. To Hirsch the mystic, and Ransom the disciplined professor, Tate added an entirely new intellectual ingredient—youthful rebellion joined with a sympathy for poetic experimentation. As yet he was a rebel with too many causes, a somewhat obscure high priest of poetry as contrasted to Ransom's role as lucid philosopher.

Unlike the other young men, Tate had no secure background or identity. He was born in Winchester, Kentucky (east of Lexington), in 1899, making him eleven years younger than Ransom. Yet, according to Tate's later memory, he grew up under the illusion that he had been born in Fairfax County, Virginia, among aristocratic maternal relatives and not in the hills of a philistine Kentucky, an illusion forced upon him by his mother and found out only at age thirty. His father was a cold, aloof, perhaps psychologically crippled Kentucky lumber entrepreneur, with his main home and business in Ashland, Kentucky, or just across the river from Ohio and down river from Huntington, West Virginia. If Tate had a home, Ashland was it, and notably one as much northern as southern. His father slowly dissipated the family holdings and, in a severe blow for young Tate, lost his business and fortune about 1915, just before Tate had to enter college. By then, the marriage of Tate's parents had degenerated into a distant toleration, as both parents tried to avoid each other as much as possible. Tate, the youngest of three sons, became an emotional captive of an exceedingly neurotic mother who lived, in Tate's words, out of her trunk, as she moved from one resort to another or spent months visiting her Virginia or Washington, D.C. relatives. She lived in the past, a romantic past largely made up of her avowedly patrician ancestors, and, indeed, she did descend from several distinguished Virginia families. Born Eleanor Varnell, she was related to the Lewis family (of the Lewis and Clark expedition), and her mother had been born a Bogan, a family that provided the prototype for the key character — Major Lewis Buchan — in Tate's later novel, *The Fathers*. His mother was born at, or near, the old Bogan family mansion of Pleasant Hill, a mansion that, like the one in the novel, was burned by Yankees during the Civil War. As a boy, Tate treasured letters, even a collection of Edgar Allan Poe, handed down from his Bogan ancestors.

Among the summer resorts frequented by the Tate family was Estill Springs, near Sewanee and Monteagle in the Cumberland Mountains of Tennessee. At this popular summering spot for Nashvillians, Allen's older brothers, Varnell and Ben, made the personal contacts that led them to attend Vanderbilt, in the pre–World War I years when Tate family fortunes still blossomed. Donald Davidson became a friend of the brothers. And Allen, from 1906 to 1908, spent time periodically in Nashville, and for three months attended a local school. His schooling was chaotic, as he moved around with his mother. He studied Latin in a private academy in Louisville and went to high schools in Evansville, Indiana, and in Ashland. In 1916 he began violin lessons in the Cincinnati Conservatory (his brother Ben became a successful businessman in Cincinnati). The next year he completed preparation for Vanderbilt at a private academy. Religiously, Tate found no clear guidelines in his own family. By his memory, he grew up with no religion at all, but he attended Catholic schools and his father was a lapsed Catholic. His mother had attended a convent school in Georgetown, D.C., the model for a similar convent in *The Fathers*. A lonely child, with an outsized head, Tate read voraciously, early developing a fascination with poetry and, by the time he enrolled at Vanderbilt, was surely the most precocious nineteen-year-old on campus.

Tate barely managed the discipline needed to remain at Vanderbilt. He enjoyed challenging his professors, particularly Edwin Mims. He shocked more conventional students by his boasts about atheism and radicalism. He joined the Fugitive group, not as a deferential undergraduate but as a cocky, at times arrogant protagonist. He also contributed a final ingredient—a familiarity with all the new, often ephemeral, schools of poetry, including the most avant-garde. Tate soon made T. S. Eliot his hero and celebrated formal experimentation. An irritant as much as a companion, he strained the tolerance of the group, but his radical proclivities alone made possible a wide-ranging discussion of modern poetry. The magical ingredients—the mixture of brilliant personalities, even an element of intellectual tension—were now all in place.[9]

Early in 1922 Hirsch urged the young men to publish some of their poems. Throughout the country small poetry magazines seemed to sprout almost monthly, so why not one in Nashville? According to later memories, Stevenson suggested the title of *Fugitive* but drew the title from one of Hirsch's poems. It is not clear what, if any, meaning the group intended by it. A fugitive, one who flees from justice or from danger, is often a wanderer, perhaps an outcast. Some assumed a connection to Hirsch, to the diaspora of Jews. The more likely meaning was their intended escape from an older sentimentality. In the preface of the first *Fugitive* number, in April 1922, Ransom said the Fugitive "flees from nothing faster than from the high-caste Brahmins of the Old South," but gave no clues as to exactly what he had in mind. The group hired a Negro printer, in a small shop, to print the first edition and set about trying to gain subscribers. Despite optimistic claims in the magazines, it would never sell well and was often on the brink of financial disaster. In the first two numbers the poets assumed humorous and revealing pseudonyms—Ransom was "Roger Prim"; Davidson, "Robin Gallovant"; Tate, "Henry Feathertop"; Hirsch, for his one contribution, "L. Oafer." By issue three, in the fall of 1922, the authors now proudly came forward and identified themselves. By then critical praise insured the continuation of their venture; the December issue contained an explanation of how the magazine began and how it functioned, plus an editorial by Tate.[10]

By December 1922 *The Fugitive* gained three new contributor-editors. After the first number, Merrill Moore, an undergraduate poet and, along with Tate, an editor of the campus humor magazine, *The Jade,* submitted a poem for the second number and very quickly joined in the discussions. Moore, the son of John Trotwood Moore, a much venerated Middle Tennessee poet, quickly became the most prolific member of the group. He was a born poet, later writing up to 100,000 sonnets while he pursued a very busy career as a Boston psychiatrist. Moore never became deeply involved in subsequent critical arguments. He strove for pure poetry, one tied to no theory. He turned poems out at a phenomenal speed, writing several sonnets in a single setting. The other poets had small success in disciplining his verse; he usually responded to criticism of one poem by writing and submitting ten more. The other additions were cousins—Ridley and Jesse Wills. Ridley, a popular but controversial and irrepressible student journalist at Vanderbilt before the war, came back in 1922 to complete his degree. A prankster of a sort, he roomed with Tate. Jesse had come to Vanderbilt with an Army training unit in 1918, and stayed on as a civilian to earn his degree. He would soon join his businessman father as a rising young executive in the National Life and Accident Insurance Company. He was a quite gifted poet, whose skills Tate always proclaimed. He also helped very much in the early promotion of *The Fugitive*. [11]

The Fugitives never tried to form a new poetic school. Their views varied too much for this, while the editorial process helped camouflage their differences. The uniformity led some to the false conclusion that Ransom wrote all the poems. Each contributor brought mimeographed poems to the Saturday evening discussions, read them aloud, and then the whole seminar acted as a very tough editorial board. The group interaction was vital, not only for the Fugitives but as a model for the later Agrarians. For the next fifty years, several participants would look back on the Fugitive years as the highlight of their lives. In 1956, Davidson remembered "the best conversation and intimate intercourse that I've ever enjoyed in my life." By 1975, Tate judged that never had "so much talent, knowledge, and character" ever assembled "in one American place at one time." The seminar provided each poet a critical but appreciative audience, forced the effort needed to write so many poems, and gave crucial support for all the work involved in preparing the publication.

By force of personality, and by their more self-conscious even though still developing theories about poetry, Ransom and Tate had the largest critical impact. They helped insure that *The Fugitive* would exemplify careful craftsmanship. In fact, its poems struck many readers as much too intricate or too cerebral. Most poems, save Tate's, remained rather conventional in meter and rhyme even when they involved a somber or satirical content. For one versed in romantic poetry, *The Fugitive* poems seemed difficult to read, uninspired and uninspiring in content. Thus, to the larger public, at Vanderbilt or in Nashville, the poems often seemed puzzling, dense, even a deliberate affront to intelligibility. Actually, most were intelligible but often required care and work on the part of readers. Tate's were often so packed and dense that even he had difficulty explaining their meaning. Nashville newspaper reviewers never developed much understanding or appreciation for the poems, but Nashvillians soon rejoiced in the critical success of the little journal. Thus, in a proprietary sense, they were proud of their Fugitives and gave honor and respect to them. So did Edwin Mims, who never liked their style of poetry but rejoiced in the prestige that soon accrued to his department from the magazine and then from the spinoff volumes of poetry published by his two colleagues, Ransom and Davidson.[12]

The Fugitive continued publication through 1925, for four volumes. Its peak years were 1923 and 1924. Because of numerous European admirers or contacts (Robert Graves and two expatriates, the Arkansas imagist John Gould Fletcher and T. S. Eliot), *The Fugitive* gained an early and appreciative foreign audience. Tate eventually developed several New York City contacts. In the second volume the editors were able to announce a hundred-dollar general prize, and a fifty-dollar prize given by Ward-Belmont College for the best poem by a coed. Despite the number of poetry magazines, hundreds of frustrated poets submitted their entries. Outside judges had a hard time agreeing on winners, but the contest further established the reputation of *The Fugitive.* By the second volume, it also contained a few poems by outside contributors, including some of the first published poems by Hart Crane. Because of its high standards of craftsmanship, its aversion to ideology, and the sheer talent of its poets, *The Fugitive* soon gained a uniquely lofty status among small poetry journals, a status reinforced later by the careers of Ransom, Tate, Davidson, and Moore.[13]

The Fugitives suffered, or gained, from some rather threatening tensions. By 1923 their sessions featured extended critical arguments. Personal antipathies flowered but never fractured the group. One blurred division involved strain between the poets committed to a career in literature (Tate, Ransom, Davidson) and those who, in a sense, were amateurs (Moore, Stevenson, Elliott, and Jesse Wills). The often intricate critical arguments of Tate and Ransom soared above the interest or capabilities of many contributors. The formal experimentation of Tate, or the packed densities and obscurities of his poems, offended the more traditional members of the group, and at times even Davidson. Tate, often arrogant in his judgments, righteous in his commitment to quality and to art, threatened to resign from the group rather than bend standards to accommodate weak poems by Frank or Hirsch. At times Tate became disillusioned with most of the circle and wrote scathing critiques of their poetry to the milder Davidson. A persistent problem, beyond finances, was getting someone to do the editorial work. After the first volume, and against the wishes of Ransom, the group formally organized and elected informal editors, with Davidson taking the job for 1923, Tate assisting. Ransom wanted to adhere to a policy of equality, with all listed equally.[14]

In 1923 a young, red-haired undergraduate from the nearby Kentucky border town of Guthrie, one Robert Penn Warren, first submitted a poem to the demanding seminar. He joined the editorial board for the final two volumes. Warren roomed with Tate and Ridley Wills in 1923, creating as bizarre a three musketeers as ever gathered on the Vanderbilt campus. He used his two years with the Fugitives as an unexcelled apprenticeship in literature. But Warren remained an apprentice; his poems revealed only a hint of his later success as both poet and novelist. Even for Tate the Fugitive years were apprenticeship years — only a few of his more mature poems appeared in *The Fugitive*, and at its termination in 1925 he was still almost as confused about his identity, as tentative and obscure in his critical stance, as he had been when he came to Vanderbilt. Davidson, the lyrical balladeer of the group, was much swayed by Ransom and by his closest lifelong friend, Tate. Always a bit awed by the intellectuality of the group, so happy to be part of it (this was his taste of utopia), Davidson experimented with more complex forms and subjects, and in retrospect received more critical acclaim for his early Fugitive poems than for later ones that were simpler, more lyrical, and also more didactic. For Ransom the Fugitive years were critical for his poetry and at least laid the basis of his later critical theory. Tate pushed him as no one ever had, forcing constant reevaluation and new refinements in his poetry. Ransom completed almost all his major poems in the Fugitive years. He was now mature and his years of poetic composition were about over. Thus, the Fugitive enterprise guided the final maturation of Ransom as a poet, forced Tate to the brink of his poetic efforts, offered a rich apprenticeship to Warren, and pulled a somewhat reluctant Davidson into some critically acclaimed experimentation. Given the significance of these men in subsequent American literary history, these modest claims take on their full significance. [15]

Even by 1923 the Fugitive group began to break up. The early volumes included Elliott and Frierson only as editors in absentia. Jesse Wills and Alec Stevenson were increasingly absorbed in business. In 1923, Curry took a leave to complete his book on Chaucer and ceased to have any role in the discussions. Moore entered the demanding Medical School. Tate, beset by what seemed to be tuberculosis, had to break off his senior year in college in 1922. He sought restored health in the North Carolina mountains and kept up his Fugitive contacts by what became a lifelong habit — long and carefully crafted letters. Back at Vanderbilt for the spring semester of 1923, he then left Nashville for good in the summer of 1924, to teach briefly in West Virginia and then to launch a difficult career as free-lance writer in New York City. He practically withdrew from the Fugitive circle. By then the problem of editorship caused new strains within the group. Ransom, because of his seniority and national reputation, gained the most professionally from the group. Critics saw him as a mentor to the group, the real editor, and often offended the other authors by so characterizing the journal. Ransom was not unaware or unconcerned about the professional side of the enterprise, and never quite went far enough in setting the record straight. Yet Davidson did more of the actual work than Ransom. Neither young professor had a Ph.D., and with poetry as their only publications they were struggling up the academic ladder. To his credit, Mims helped win Ransom his full professorship, and after his first published volumes of poems at least raised Davidson to the austere rank of assistant professor. But Ransom, never a workaholic, had to give most of his time to campus duties.

A final threat to the earlier harmony involved Ransom's and Tate's fight over critical standards. Tate took offense at a Ransom slighting of Eliot's "Waste Land" (too lacking in structure) in the July 1923 *Literary Review*. For Tate, who had just adopted Eliot as his greatest literary god, this was a form of treason. At the time, he already had a love-hate relationship to Ransom, at times valuing him as a mentor, at times resenting him as an authority figure. Tate, typically, wrote a sharp letter to the *Review*, lambasting Ransom's views. He wrote as if a disinterested reader, one who scarcely knew Ransom or his poetry. Ransom was stung, angered. He wrote Tate that he "shouldn't do these things," and tried, with great patience, to clarify his problems with "The Waste Land" (no mature philosophy, a first transcript of experience, not enough head to govern heart, a young man not yet up to poetry). He composed, but did not publish, a sharp rebuttal to Tate's letter, one in which he clarified his former friendship. His reaction hurt Tate, who was much more sensitive and vulnerable than Ransom. Davidson helped mediate, and within a year the two were exchanging critical comments on each other's poems. Later they became the closest of friends. A disciplined, prudent Ransom knew how much he gained from Tate's criticism, and Ransom was not one to hold a grudge. Tate was generous to a fault toward other writers. But he did not forget or fully forgive Ransom. He later admitted that his letter was insolent and ill-advised, but he still rejoiced when, much later, Ransom reversed himself on Eliot, if not on that one poem. Even in a final memorial, Tate still remembered Ransom as too cold and calculating, and admitted that as a student he never liked him. So passionate himself, the calm demeanor of Ransom infuriated.[16]

Beyond such manageable tensions, the Fugitives faced grave financial problems by 1924. A hopeful business agent who financed Volume Three lost a considerable amount of money and could not continue support. *The Fugitive* clearly had to have a managing editor to go on. Ransom again strenuously objected to an elected editor. But he relented in 1925, since he joined Warren on the masthead as "Editors serving for 1925." Warren did most of the work for the final volume, now published only quarterly.[17]

The final numbers listed one additional editor-contributor—Laura Riding Gottschalk—but one who was unable to function as part of the seminar, itself now almost defunct. Riding (her professional name) had entered the first poetry contest, won a rave review from one judge and effusive praise from several of the Fugitives, led by Tate. She rejoiced in the honor and the recognition, worked hard but unsuccessfully to sell subscriptions, and contributed several poems to the final two volumes. She was able to meet with her fellow Fugitives only once in Nashville. She came with such great hopes. She had no money, no outlet for her poems, no support. Thus she invested too much in the cause. As an outsider, she found the other Fugitives cold and formal toward her. They meant no discourtesy, but as an established in-group were not about to capitulate to her charms. She misinterpreted their motives, became disillusioned, plagued the final editors with too many sloppy poems, and by gossip in 1927 almost, and perhaps deliberately, tried to fan a new fight between Tate and Ransom. Soon the group despaired of her, although at least Tate bent over backward to help befriend her in times of need. He felt that he had discovered her and for a time predicted her poetry as the strongest of the group. He viewed her and Hart Crane as, potentially, the most powerful poets in America. Tate also helped gain her a new patron in Robert Graves. Then, to the despair of the old-fashioned moralists in the group (most of them), Laura not only joined Graves in England, but was soon off on a then scandalous, clearly adulterous tour up the Nile.

By the end of 1925 it was evident that *The Fugitive* had to suspend publication. It was again solvent, but too few of the Fugitives were able to contribute either poems or work. Even in 1924 several members had wanted to suspend publication, Ransom included. In 1925 most contributors were too busy with their various careers to contribute. At the end of the year Warren had to leave Vanderbilt to attend graduate school at the University of California. Hirsch and Frank, although willing hosts, did not have the talent to do the editorial work. The most able and the most overworked local supporter was Davidson, who had an enormous personal stake in the community of poets and, emotionally, never accepted the demise of the journal. He could not do it all. The final 1925 number announced suspension, not because of financial strain but the lack of a sacrificial editor. [18]

The suspension of publication did not mean an end to the Fugitive circle. Dispersion and the demands of other careers had already reduced attendance at the weekly seminars. Too few Fugitives were in the area or had enough time to write even one poem every two weeks. Yet the group continued to reassemble frequently in the late twenties and on rare occasions up until 1962. Any time two or three of the scattered Fugitives returned to Nashville, or important outside poets visited, the local contingent tried to plan an evening meeting, one that followed the old format. Each person was still expected to read a poem and face the criticism of the group. Even after James Frank died in 1944, other Nashville Fugitives, particularly Stevenson and Jesse Wills, hosted the rare meetings.

In 1926, Donald Davidson began planning an anthology of the best Fugitive poems. This was his substitute for the earlier meetings, his way of holding on to the group. His success in gaining a publisher for his own poems emboldened him to approach a publisher. Tate, with the needed New York contacts, helped to gain a contract with Harcourt Brace. An overworked Davidson had to do all the unexpectedly hard work. It soon became apparent that most of the Fugitives wanted to include not only the best of their Fugitive poems, but either new ones written after 1925 or poems either written or published before 1925 in other journals. Davidson not only had to struggle with permissions, but to make hard, often offending decisions about which poems to include. Laura Riding was especially sensitive and demanding. During the preparation process, the local Fugitives met at least once in a regular evening seminar, and a few met informally to help make editorial decisions. The book was well received and, because of the new poems, constituted the final published product of the Fugitive circle.[19]

After 1930 it is important to distinguish the Fugitives from the Agrarians. The Fugitives, by choice, welcomed ideologically diverse people who shared an interest in poetry. They formed a single interest club. The long, complex discussions centered mainly on poetry or on literary subjects. Left muted were broader philosophical and political commitments. Not that these could be entirely separate from critical issues, or even from the content of poems, but that the group was able to keep these concerns peripheral to their seminars, else the group might not have lasted long enough to produce poems. Only four Fugitives became Agrarians, although two other

Agrarians (Fletcher and Andrew Lytle) attended at least one Fugitive seminar and contributed poems to *The Fugitive*. But the later eminence of the Agrarian four tended to obscure the fact that eleven other Fugitives either had no interest in Agrarianism or, as in the case of Elliott, openly repudiated it. The distinction remained clear within the two groups. A Fugitive meeting, even in the early thirties, was a poetry seminar, not a place to plot Agrarian conspiracies.

Superficially, one might even view the Fugitives as ideological opposites of the later Agrarians. After all, the early Fugitives repudiated the sentimentality of a lost cause, eschewed Southern themes for their poetry, and gained almost all readers and all respect outside the South. Except for Tate, they did not pose either as rebels or assertive modernists, whatever meaning one gives to those loaded labels. But, for the South, their poetry seemed quite defiant and daring.

Little in the papers of the Fugitives gives credence to any deliberate antisouthern strategy. It is as if the South, or their southern identity, was never at stake, not a matter of self-consciousness. Under the guidance of Ransom, they became focally involved with the technical problems of poetry and selected deliberately diffuse subjects that allowed them to experiment with technique. That is, they wanted to avoid images easily associated with deep loyalties and sentiments and to avoid any political or religious partisanship. Such issues diverted one from the formal problems of the art. In so far as they identified themselves as southern, their goal was to learn how to be the best possible poets by cosmopolitan standards. If they achieved their goal, then, in a sense, this would be an achievement for the South in the same sense as a southerner who excelled as a scientist or a scholar. It was better to be a good poet than a southern poet. Some of the young men, particularly Stevenson, Moore and Davidson, chafed under such narrowed, technical, academic restrictions. Even had they rebelled, *The Fugitive,* given over to the brief, necessarily dense poems made mandatory by the multiple contributors to each volume, was not an appropriate medium either for poetic epics or sentimental local color.

Contrary to a later myth, Ransom, Davidson, and Tate did not discover the South about 1925. Their correspondence includes several references to southern issues in the early twenties. Ransom and

Tate did not then find, and would never find, poetry an appropriate medium for addressing such issues. Davidson did not quite agree and, after 1925, broke deliberately from what he then saw as the overly restrictive Fugitive mold. What is clear before 1925 is that none of these three men had made any strong commitment to the South, old or new. In fact, the evidence points the other way. Ransom desperately wanted a teaching position in a prestigious northern university. Tate, embittered by his experiences at Vanderbilt, almost fled to New York City by 1924 and at first rejoiced in a type of liberation. He was, as always, ambivalent, confused about his identity. But it is notable that in 1922, when ill in the mountains of North Carolina, Tate had only contempt for the local residents, for a land the Lord forgot, for ignorant, self-satisfied clannish people, with less sensibility than the fish in the rivers. Perhaps such mountain folk were not typical of the South. But he soon felt rejected by the South as a whole, for the rest of his life denied any great artistic tradition in the South, long nourished an image of southerners as parochials (more so than the people in Timbuktu), and so rejoiced in the tolerance of New York, where no one asked if you were a virgin or drank liquor, that he vowed never to return to Nashville.[20] Davidson had more home loyalties. When in the Army, he vowed never to live long outside the South, for "It is my country." But even he married a Yankee, sought a newspaper job in Cleveland, and long contemplated a career in Ohio. In no sense was he a professional southerner or even very defensive about the South before 1925.[21]

Later, after they became deeply committed to the South, both Tate and Davidson tried to explain their tactics as Fugitive poets. In a sense, Tate argued that only new poetic techniques could serve the cause of the South he came to admire, a South that once embodied a deeply traditional culture. The literature of the lost cause, of moonlight and magnolias, or of local color, was not only false to the fact and exploitative of the South, but was a literature produced for northern markets. The older poetic techniques, tied to Victorian sensibilities, were inadequate for the task of rescuing the real South. Taking most of his cues from T. S. Eliot, he thus made the technical cause of poetic experimentation one with the largely political cause of restoring a traditional, religious society. Had the

Fugitives written the sentimental, undisciplined, indulgent, moralistic poetry craved by Mims, they would thereby have joined the progressive, New South crowd, or those who had already capitulated to alien values. Implicit in this argument was the need for contemporary poets to express, as honestly as possible, the typical experience of moderns, an experience of confusion, rootlessness, and alienation. The truth could not be simple or flattering. Tate never repudiated this view, although as a seeker after redemption he later tried, as did Eliot, to uncover a philosophical or theological ground behind all the modern confusions. He never made a mythical South a subject of his poetry. Unfortunately his most famous poem, in a sense his "Waste Land," and a poem he spent a lifetime perfecting, "An Ode to the Confederate Dead," seemed by its very title to deny this. The title was ironic. The poem was not really an ode at all, but a devastating commentary on the alienation of modern humanity from its past.[22]

Davidson took a very different tack. First of all, he repudiated, not the poetry in *The Fugitive,* but the narrow orthodoxy that Ransom urged upon the young poets. He soon realized that he should write poetry that was natural to him, that he really liked, but a poetry that fit no formula. His early poetry was indeed sincere and often powerful, but he soon saw it as too complex, too fastidious, too difficult. Also, its classical themes, its universal symbols were unnecessarily remote from the rhythms of southern life. Surely the Fugitives could have moved closer to home without falling prey to sentimentality or escapist forms of local color. After 1925, Davidson tried to find such a middle way, often to the despair of Ransom and Tate, who saw too much moralism and escapism in his lyrical celebration of Tennessee frontiersmen in his second volume of poems, *The Tall Men.* Davidson admitted that such had been the exploitation of the Old South theme that no respectable poet could even attempt a poem on Lee (he later attempted just this). But this did not mean that writers could not exploit materials all around them without becoming narrowly provincial. Given this taste for local subject matter, however, and a broader treatment, Davidson could sympathize with Tate. He agreed that new techniques, or the relaxation of formal constraints, might be necessary for an honest southern poetry. Nevertheless, to him, the poetry had to be loyal to the southern tradition, and soon he was alone among the former Fugitives in demanding an almost ideological test for southern writers.[23]

Davidson, even before 1925, rejoiced at a revival of letters in the South. He already believed that the South was the one part of the country most likely to produce great literature. Thus, even though the Fugitives did not write about the South, they nonetheless became prime exhibits in his thesis. The South produced them. That they were not self-consciously southern in the early twenties only testified to the fact that they were at ease within a familiar and traditional society. They had no identity problems to struggle with or to divide them. They were, as Davidson put it, all cousins, part of a clan, with most basic issues already settled, agreed upon, consensual. Thus, the Fugitives could quickly become a close community. They knew who they were, even if the occasion did not yet require a defense of that identity. No one was attacking it. He believed such a harmonious, creative group was inconceivable in a more heterogeneous society. The gathering of young men in New York City could only lead to ideological disagreement, identity clashes, and thus more political struggle than artistic creativity. Neither Hirsch nor Tate would seem to fit this familial image.

Davidson never repudiated this argument. In a critical essay on Tate, he tried to assimilate him to the thesis. For Tate's poetry sprang from a conviction born from historical fact, his belonging to a "truly ordered and humane society." The modernist aspects of his poetry reflected only his integrity, his attempt to tell the truth about his age, to achieve a clear and full, and thus tragic, vision, and to do it in a medium fully his own, not borrowed or inauthentic. Typically, Davidson argued that Tate, in the context of his short, tight, packed poems, nonetheless achieved the weight and dignity of epic poems, even as Tate argued that the modern age allowed no epic poetry.[24]

In the midst of the Agrarian enthusiasm of the early thirties, the Fugitives met on occasion, as during a visit by John Gould Fletcher in May 1933. Such gatherings, strictly for poetry, remained quite distinct from the political and economic agitation of the Agrarians and thus included local poets and businessmen who rejected the Agrarian gospel. By the late thirties such occasional meetings seemed to have ended, only to resume again in the fifties.

By World War II, the growing fame of Ransom, Tate, and Warren seemed to elevate the historical importance of the earlier Fugitives. Even people at Vanderbilt began to value the heritage. In March 1943, A. F. Kuhlman, director of the Joint University Libraries (the unified library system owned by Vanderbilt and George Peabody College for Teachers), asked key members of the Fugitive and Agrarian groups to cooperate in creating a Fugitive-Agrarian collection. Technically, the JUL was not a part of Vanderbilt, but both Tate and Davidson interpreted this as a gesture from Vanderbilt. For both, the gesture raised old resentments. Tate, at first flattered by even this gesture, was inclined to cooperate. But not for long. He heard rumors that someone in a high position at Vanderbilt accused him of soliciting such a collection to boost his own prestige. One senses that Tate looked for an excuse, for he had a love-hate relationship to Vanderbilt. In high huff, he refused to give any of his papers to Vanderbilt and soon deposited them at Princeton. He aired all his grievances with Vanderbilt, which he described as "an institution which combines the qualities of a whorehouse and a graveyard. Mims is the Madam, and Carmichael [Oliver C., the new Vanderbilt Chancellor] is the sexton." Plaintively, he argued that he was not a disgrace to Vanderbilt University, and the attitude of the people down there "has been just that." After listing all the universities at which he had lectured, he noted that he had never been formally called to speak before any Vanderbilt group. Yet, in his travels, almost everyone identified him with Vanderbilt or even asked him when he had last taught there. He considered submitting a bill to Vanderbilt for his unappreciated services.[25]

Davidson would eventually cooperate and give a rich collection of papers to Vanderbilt. But not at that time, and not before he aired his own bitterness. Despite twenty-one years of creative activity, all to the credit and benefit of Vanderbilt, he had heretofore received no institutional support or recognition. No official at Vanderbilt had suggested that his work had any value at all. He had belatedly, and begrudgingly, received promotions, but other Fugitives, such as Warren, did not even get this much. As writers, the

Fugitives had received no institutional support, and the majority had moved to other universities that did appreciate their work. He noted that only once, in twenty-three years, had the university asked him to address the students in chapel. Ransom did it only once. Tate had been ostracized. He doubted that there was "a single spontaneous written expression from a chancellor or other high official at Vanderbilt University which indicated regard or approval for what we had done." He would not then give his papers, for such would be a humiliation, a denial of all that he believed in. He doubted that his rejected brothers, Tate, Warren, and Ransom, would give their papers to Vanderbilt (none ever did). Given to self-pity, Davidson concluded his response to Kuhlman: "No human power, indeed, can restore to me the lost and injured years which I can call to mind. By no earthly means can the old Fugitive group be brought back."[26]

Largely through the initiative of the English department, with funds from the Rockefeller Foundation and the support of the American Studies Association, Vanderbilt hosted a Fugitive Reunion in 1956. Ten Fugitives attended. Frank, Johnson, and Frierson were already deceased; Curry, Riding, and Ridley Wills were unable to attend. In the next year, both Moore and Alfred Starr would die. The Fugitives gathered in four nonpublic sessions but, unfortunately for the fullest fellowship, in sessions attended by a few of the inevitable parasites of artistic creativity—scholars. Very quickly, the participants fell into their old roles, even an ailing Sidney Hirsch, who came to only one session. Technically, these were not Fugitive meetings. No one read new poems for mutual criticism, but the discussions soon went beyond nostalgic memories. The old divisions over poetic standards reappeared, with a somewhat anachronistic debate between traditionalists and modernists. The reunion had a magical effect. Tate, apprehensive before the meeting, ended up the most enthused. The Reunion, he said, "affected me deeply. Since May 5th there have been moments when I felt I would like to come back."[27]

From 1956 until death began to decimate their ranks, the Fugitives continued to meet together. In 1958, William Y. Elliott was able to get five or six Fugitives together at Harvard at the time of a visit by John Crowe Ransom. Then, the Vanderbilt English de-

The surviving Fugitives at the 1956 Reunion at Vanderbilt (Tate, Ransom, and Davidson in front row; Starr, Stevenson, and Warren in middle row; Elliott, Moore, Jesse Wills, and Hirsch in rear)

partment began to hold annual Literary Symposia, with prominent speakers, often Fugitives. These became the occasion for other Fugitive reunions. Ransom returned to Vanderbilt to teach for the fall semester of 1961–62. Before he left in January, several Fugitives gathered for a reunion. Ransom read from an older poem. Both Alec Stevenson and Jesse Wills wrote new poems for the occasion. Davidson read from a novel he was then writing.

The last significant gathering of the Fugitives occurred in April 1962, in conjunction with a Literary Symposium. Both Tate and Ransom came, with Tate as a featured speaker. Ransom even tried to prepare a new poem; he ended up rewriting an older one and, in Tate's opinion, completely ruined it. Tate struggled with a new poem. Thus they tried to adhere to the old rules. Yet, by then, only six of the original poets were able to attend (Warren did not come). Never again would Tate, Davidson, and Ransom join in such a meeting. Now old men, they realized that this might be the end. Tate wrote that it had been perfect, and then asked, "Shall we ever be on the same program again? I feel the most should be made of every reunion lest it be the last." It was.[28]

II.

In Defense
of the South

In 1925 everyone at Vanderbilt began talking about the South. Regional self-consciousness seemed inescapable in the year of the Scopes Trial. In December, John Crowe Ransom reported that evolution was a hot subject on campus. The one Vanderbilt philosophy professor on campus, Herbert Sanborn, a disciple of Borden Parker Bowne, Methodism's greatest philosopher, led an attack against Darwin and his modernist defenders. Edwin Mims pushed to completion his book, *The Advancing South,* a celebration of southern progress despite the atavistic fundamentalists at Dayton. The sharp caricatures of Mencken and other northern reporters placed most southerners on the defensive, but at odds as to the correct strategy for a counterattack. Before the year was out, both Ransom and Davidson had joined the debates. Possibly for the first time in their lives, they began to think seriously about the problems of an impoverished South and to explore the southern component of their own identity. Up in New York City, with more intensity, and much more personally at stake, Allen Tate also discovered the South, both as a problem and as a possible solution to all his confusions.

In less than two years all three young men became avid defenders of one or another South. In 1927 they began coordinating their strategies in such a defense, and first talked of a book of essays as one component of such a defense. This would become, in 1930, *I'll*

Take My Stand. In the preceding three years, they clarified and matured their own views about the South, old and new; cultivated
areas of overlap in their doctrines; and searched for and then recruited some fellow travelers. Their first achievement was almost entirely literary—a series of articles and reviews culminating in *I'll
Take My Stand.* But the book, and the rapidly changing economy,
helped produce, by 1933, a loosely organized Agrarian movement.
To understand the origins of the book and the movement, one has
to deal with the quite different paths each of these three young men
took to what they eventually called Agrarianism.

Davidson took the first steps. He also made a deep, unswerving
commitment to the South, not as an ideal but as a living actuality.
Such came easy to him, without all the philosophical and religious
complications that marked the commitments of Ransom and Tate.
Home loyalties ran deep in Davidson. Mencken's barbs hurt him
personally, as if a beloved family member had been assaulted. He
had absorbed as a child the epic story of the heroic South defeated
in its bid for independence and then cursed by Federal occupation
and black rule. Thus, he already identified strongly with the Confederate cause. So, shortly, would Tate. These two young men were
only two generations removed from that war. Their grandfathers
had eaten of the grapes of wrath. The grandsons' teeth were now
on edge. Davidson, as a child, heard stories of the war and the agonies of federal occupation from a live-in grandmother. His family
had been friends of Nathan Bedford Forrest. In 1925 the northern
attack on the South revived all these memories and required him
in all honor to challenge once again another Yankee invasion.[1]

In 1925, as in most years, Davidson suffered from overwork. He
came close to depression, felt unhappy and, disheartened by the
breakup of the Fugitive circle, vainly sought some new challenge.
With only an M.A., he seemed stymied professionally and always
felt unappreciated. In 1924, with the publication of his first book
of poems, *An Outland Piper,* he had gained a promotion to assistant professor in the English department, at a still measly salary of
$2,200. He had small prospects for further promotions unless he
could publish something scholarly. Thus, he was looking for a subject and at least by 1926 sought a book topic relating to southern
literature. He needed money to meet family expectations. Not at

all extravagant, he nonetheless tried to live comfortably, with books, travel, and domestic help in his home. His wife had taken the time and money to gain a degree in law and by 1925 had a job in the Law School. Still, Davidson could barely stay solvent. Thus, in 1924 he had taken on a second job as editor of the book page of the *Nashville Tennessean*. Later, he was able to syndicate his column, and the outstanding reviews he solicited from literary friends, in other southern newspapers. This eventually raised his pay to $200 a month, or as much as he gained from his heavy teaching load at Vanderbilt (mostly Freshman English). In the next six years he personally reviewed over four hundred books, gained national attention for the quality of his reviewers, and did as much or more than anyone else to enhance the cultural life of Nashville. But the higher pay was still ahead in 1925, and thus he considered leaving Vanderbilt. Tate explored job possibilities for him at Columbia University, and Davidson seemed quite willing to move. He admitted fears of New York City, stressed his allegiance to the South, but had to seek financial independence. In fact, neither Columbia nor any other university could match his combined income from two jobs and his wife's salary.[2]

Early in 1926, Mims published his upbeat response to Dayton, *The Advancing South*. Davidson, Ransom, and Tate all read it critically, and each tried to develop and eventually publish his response. Davidson was most impressed, most generous in his early comments. Underlying the book's optimism was Mims's contention that the South, despite such setbacks as lynchings or the embarrassing display of the fundamentalists, had already made tremendous strides, and that progress, not reaction, best characterized its recent past. Implicit in this was a claim that the South was slowly catching up with the North in industrial growth, educational facilities, and even artistic achievement. Thus Mims accepted the values of the critics, whereas Tate and Ransom wanted to challenge just these assumptions. Actually, Mims's analysis was more subtle than a resentful Tate could ever concede. Typical of other New South cheerleaders, he noted distinctive and desirable cultural traits in the South, not the least being a pervasive religiosity that appealed to the evangelical Mims. But he believed southerners had to face up to deep social and economic problems, get rid of any blind optimism, eschew any escape into the mystique of a lost cause, and then, by a very selective and intelligent borrowing of northern and English techniques, set about the laborious task of reform. Although Mims advocated black progress along with white and fought against lynching or overt repression, even he could not accept social equality for blacks. Ironically, his approach to racial issues very closely paralleled that taken by Robert Penn Warren in *I'll Take My Stand*.[3]

Davidson eventually published his response to the Scopes Trial, and to Mims's book, in an essay in the *Forum* in 1928. By the time it appeared, it no longer reflected his earlier belligerent views. The essay revealed Davidson at his best—generous, undogmatic, subtle. He disarmed critics by pointing to the diversity of the South. Already absorbed in the study of both southern history and literature, he knew the South's sharp contrasts—Billy Sunday revivals and meetings of the American Association for the Advancement of Science, ancestral mansions and gaudy gasoline stations, ancient homesteads and rayon mills, leisurely aristocrats and rowdy frontiersmen, Charleston and Birmingham, Virginia and Texas, mountains and delta. But he did, in a sense, defend the fundamentalists. They placed morally serious roadblocks to the new age, asked how far science, which serves human physical needs, should also determine one's philosophy. But, despite moral fervor, they tried to save youth in ways that hastened their apostasy, even as antievolution laws were straw barriers against a great wind. Inevitably, intellectual progress would spill out from southern universities.

Then southerners would have to face the hard question—what type of progress did they want? How far should the South submit to novelty, energy, quantity? Borrowing themes from Joseph Wood Krutch's *Modern Temper,* Davidson asked whether it should give up repose, noblesse oblige, romantic love, beauty, good manners, and a belief in God. Clearly, he thought not. He preferred slow change at best. He feared the role of businessmen, the masters of industrial expansion, the boosters in local Chambers of Commerce, who would probably have the last word in the South's future. They tended to ignore Dayton, but not efforts to get child labor laws. The South would do well to resist their progress, to avoid such new problems as strikes, agitators, wage slavery, graft, and monopoly prices. Actually, his outlook was not too different from that of Mims. Da-

vidson still respected his department head and still hoped for "progressive" or melioristic answers to southern problems. He would
not fully repudiate such positions until the publication of *I'll Take
My Stand*.[4]

Whatever the solution to southern ills, Davidson from now on
would commit himself to finding them. For him, unlike both Tate
and Ransom, the South was not important because it exemplified
some philosophic ideal, some model that would have universal appeal. He loved the South for its peculiarities, for its own unique
history, for whatever heroes and ideals it had produced. This visceral, often uncritical loyalty distinguished him from Tate and Ransom. It even affected Davidson's poetry. From 1925 on, he would
self-consciously adapt his poetry to his own political goals, as he
tried to describe, at times to idealize, and always to defend his own
section or region. He had chafed at the narrow conception of poetry among the Fugitives and, with a sense of liberation, wrote his
long epic, *The Tall Men* (1927), a series of connected poems which
celebrated Tennessee pioneers. He finally let himself go, indulging
the lyricism and sensuality that he had earlier tried to suppress.
And, quite openly, he admitted his moral or political purposes. To
a friend, he described *The Tall Men*'s message—that modern southerners should hold the door against progress, that they should re-
tain "spiritual values against the fiery gnawing of industrialism."
This was the first time, on record, that Davidson used the term "industrialism" as a sweeping label for all the evils that threatened the
South. In all likelihood, he borrowed the word from his colleague
Ransom, who had by this time worked out a much more coherent,
philosophical, and deliberately reactionary program for the South.[5]

It is not easy to explain why Ransom, in a two year period, became so involved with the South. Unlike Davidson, he had displayed
no strong regional loyalties before 1925. In the Fugitive years he
seemed almost entirely absorbed in literary issues. His one reference to the evolution debate on campus indicated little more than
an intellectual interest on his part. But it is clear that he was seeking
a new direction in his professional life. In the summer of 1926 he
told Davidson that he was immersed in a lot of philosophical books.
Soon he was trying out on Tate ideas for a new book, one tentatively entitled *The Third Moment*. His plan was not directly related

to the South. Already, although he would not admit it to himself, Ransom had given up on the writing of poetry, not only because of the hard work that went into his poems but perhaps also because poetry provided a poor basis for academic success. Thus, he decided to wade into larger philosophical and critical issues, issues that involved not only the formal demands of poetry but the social and economic conditions that sustained artistic creativity. For him the problem of art always overlapped the even larger issue of religion. He always paired the two. And, at least, the evolution debate forced him to confront his own Methodist heritage.[6]

In 1926, Ransom became fully involved in his new philosophical effort. Throughout his life he periodically shifted his interests and always, at the beginning of each new phase, exuded a contagious enthusiasm, although not much passion. Committed, intellectually absorbed, reasonable, persuasive, always Ransom seemed to hold back, to keep a certain distance. Thus he remained open for later retreat, disengagement, or surrender. Then he would find another cause.

Somehow, in his Oxford years or later, Ransom had ceased to believe in the old gods of his youth. The Methodist doctrines of his family, however powerful they remained as myths, however useful in poetry, no longer seemed believable. It is not that he chose to disbelieve them. Such basic beliefs never confront one as options, open to choice. They lie back of and guide authentic choices. Ransom never fully bared his own deepest beliefs. But even this early he apparently accepted some broad and rich and religiously pregnant form of naturalism, possibly an Aristotelianism or Stoic form, one anchored to a nontheistic but metaphysical ground. He never clarified such a view, and one can only conjecture at its exact content. But in the twenties and early thirties he was not quite at ease with such a position. Possibly he felt guilt, a sense of betrayal toward his minister father. In any case, and reminiscent of William James, he wanted to defend, to give intellectual respectability to, more literal and mythical forms of relgious belief. In this sense he defended what he no longer believed. But in language reminiscent of John Dewey, he always affirmed a religious outlook, a religious attitude or stance toward life, which for him meant a type of piety or respect, awe and reverence, toward whatever powers originate

and sustain life. Much later he would publicly affirm a type of religious naturalism and humanism, to the despair of Tate, who always thirsted after a dogmatic and orthodox form of Christianity.

Throughout his Agrarian phase, Ransom struggled with religious
issues. Some ambivalences haunted him. But, more than most people, he made the issues cerebral ones and kept a degree of personal
detachment from his own theories, some of which at times seemed
rather half-baked. Tate and Davidson sensed this detachment, but
could never quite fathom Ransom and understand what lay behind
his crusades. Deep down, they could not fully trust him. He might
desert them in the midst of the battle, for he could not be a true
believer in the sense that they, by temperament, always were. At
moments Tate could become infuriated at Ransom, who seemed to
play intellectual games, who was too self-centered, too personally
ambitious, too calculating. In fact, Ransom never let his causes divert his attention for long from career goals. Whatever the enthusiasm of the moment, he assessed its marketability—would it lead to
new and profitable publications, would it gain him academic recognition, would it help him gain a promotion and a higher salary?
Tate and Davidson were not, for financial reasons could not, be
aloof from such practical issues, but they were more likely than Ransom to sacrifice themselves for a cause. They displayed a higher
courage.

In the fall of 1925, Ransom outlined the contents of a new book.
He was vague as to the details. He hoped to get a Guggenheim and
go to England, possibly there to complete a Ph.D. One should not
ignore the role of grant proposals in stimulating, or shaping, the
work of scholars. Ransom, in a letter to Robert Graves, talked vaguely
about a book on poetic irony, on nature and poetry, or the Gothic
principle in English poetry. He used Gothic as the opposite of Classic, and closely related it to religious orthodoxy and, by implication, to mythic and nonrational religions, exemplified for him by
Roman Catholicism and fundamentalism. By the end of 1925 he
saw the Gothic as rooted in the common life of ordinary people,
a type of low life counterpoint to classic rationality. From here it
erupted in artists like Shakespeare, contributing to the vitality of
literature. Religions also sprang from the same folk sources, from
the sensual or even obscene aspects of direct experience, and only

later became emasculated abstractions in the hands of theologians or "liberals" (his term). Scientists also, by compressing the rich nuances of raw experience into their conceptual abstractions, subverted both religion and poetry, for poets have to embody the colorful particularities of life, not just ideal essences or concepts. He never won his Guggenheim for such a project but begged a semester's leave from Vanderbilt. In the summer and fall of 1927, in Colorado and New Mexico (his wife, Robb Ravell, was from Denver), he tried to turn these incoherent ideas into a book.[7]

Ransom never kept the manuscript of his projected book, which publishers rejected and he eventually repudiated. But in long letters to Tate he clarified his main arguments, most of which remained integral to his 1930 book, *God Without Thunder,* to many of his Agrarian essays, and to his later critical theory. By the fall of 1926, he had expanded his earlier Gothic theme, tied closely to English literature, into a much more general philosophical thesis. But it matched a lifelong outlook. One suspects the influence of Henri Bergson, possibly William James. The basic doctrine is a now familiar one, perhaps appropriately called phenomenology. Ransom stressed the duality in human life. He began with unreflective, nonconceptualized, concrete experience, or what William James identified as pure perception. He called this the First Moment. It contrasts, at times almost violently, with the Second Moment, with the subsequent reflections back on the First Moment. In the Second Moment, humans (animals live only with the First Moment) reduce the First Moment to concepts, to abstract meanings. The game, when well played, is science. The reason to play it is practical. The criterion of success is thus pragmatic—what works. With James and Bergson, Ransom emphasized, not so much practical utility (he never denied this or its importance), but how much the cognitive abstractions subtracted from or abridged the qualitative richness of perception. The resulting abstract was not at all experienced reality, but rather a fictitious and abstract world of illusion. Influenced by Freud, Ransom speculated that the nonconceptual remainder of perception may remain in memory or be suppressed into a type of unconscious meaning. He thus referred to our "lost knowledge." The positive scientific outlet leads humans to flee from the First Moment as soon as possible and to reduce it to a conceptual transcript.

Like William James, he saw this scientific proclivity as dangerous if not kept in its proper and purely practical sphere. It so dwarfs life, leaves out so many valuable aspects of experience, as to destroy all richness and beauty.

What Ransom wanted to emphasize was a Third Moment, a way of recapturing the suppressed wholes of immediate experience. Obviously, conceptual systems cannot restore the wholeness. They only order concepts. Logic, science, ordinary philosophy are not sufficient to the task of the Third Moment. One can recover the First Moment only through contrived images, by use of the imagination and not by a logical act. Imagination, dipping into the storeroom, can bring up the lost aspects of the First Moment and allow an appropriate joy. As he had suggested in his earlier discussion of Gothic literature, this act of recovery is regressive, not progressive. But (and this was critical to Ransom) as mature humans, addicted to thought, to contemplation, we cannot go all the way back to perception. The images of the Third Moment combine aspects of raw experience—concrete, full of quality—with concepts, and thus abstract order. The Third Moment, a mixed world, has its perfect expression in art, in the marriage of experiential fullness to intellectual form, yet without losing the tension between the two. Ransom wanted the concepts utilized in art to remain at the restricted level of generality exemplified in objects (cats and dogs) and not to soar off into the supersensible realm of relational or grouping concepts. Ransom believed that the Third Moment found primitive expression in dreams, in visions, and above all in religion. These insights, not very original and never worked out with philosophical rigor, grounded all Ransom's subsequent literary criticism.[8]

This line of analysis, which scarcely required a book, led to a dead end. One suspects what often happened later to Ransom—a piling on of abstractions until he lost focus and control over his subject. He needed concrete ways of developing a thesis. Religion proved one of these and led him to his book, *God Without Thunder*. The South was a second and led to a series of essays, including one that became the opening for *I'll Take My Stand*.

Another question remains. How did Ransom move from such philosophical theories to the Old South? The answer has to be, in part, speculative. Even as he worked on his Third Moment, Ran-

Donald Davidson in 1928, as he began planning *I'll Take My Stand*

som read Spengler and, without going off on a pessimistic binge
(he never would), he began to refer more often to the ills of modern
society, as yet ills not fully described. Overt in almost all his letters
to Tate was a critique of the dehumanizing effects of applied science
and technology, of what he now called industrialism. Such themes
suggested the Old South as a convenient example of a premodern,
prescientific society, although not as full an example as late medie-
val Europe, as Tate pointed out frequently. Apparently, the possibility of making the tie to the Old South came in part out of his
ongoing dialogue with both Davidson and Tate. He had arrived at
his conception of the Old South before Davidson, in early 1927,
discussed the possibility of a book on both southern literature and
southern traditions.[9]

Tate's life was as chaotic as Ransom's and Davidson's was tran-
quil. Davidson, although beset by problems, full of complaints,
and periodically disheartened, had a stable job, a degree of financial security, a talented wife, a much indulged daughter, and a circle
of supportive friends. Ransom, although perennially in debt, lived
the life of a country gentleman. He sequestered time for sports and
games, had a very stable and private home life, adored his children
(two by 1925, one later), and had a secure professorship at Vanderbilt. Perhaps more important, both Davidson and Ransom had a
past, a clear sense of identity, home loyalties. Tate had none of this.
He yearned for it all.

Tate graduated from Vanderbilt in August 1923, magna cum laude.
Because illness had forced him to postpone the degree, he was always listed with the class of 1922. He hoped to enter a graduate
program in classical studies in the fall of 1923. Then came a bitter
disappointment. Penniless, he had to have a scholarship. Mims, as
chairman of the English department, refused to recommend him,
and this doomed his chances at Vanderbilt and probably lay behind
his subsequent failure to win a fellowship at Yale in 1924. Tate never
forgave Mims. Actually, Mims agreed to write the letter if Tate apologized for several irreverent acts during the previous years (Tate had
teased and ridiculed Mims unmercifully). Davidson, sympathizing
with proud old Mims, unsuccessfully urged such a humbling gesture from Tate, all to no avail. Whether for good or ill, this petty
incident denied Tate a normal academic career and forced him, if

he were to live up to his intense, idealistic commitment to literature, to try to live by free-lance work or editorial jobs. For years Tate tried to survive this way, with endless frustrations and periods of near starvation.[10]

Still hoping to begin graduate work in the fall of 1924, Tate taught high school in Lumberport, West Virginia, in the spring. While he was away from Vanderbilt, his beloved friend and protégé, Robert Penn Warren, suffered a severe mental breakdown, with a despair so great he attempted suicide. Tate, of course, blamed it all on Mims but took personal responsibility for helping Warren, whom he viewed as the most talented of the Fugitives. As soon as his job allowed, he rushed down to Guthrie, Kentucky, to spend much of the summer with "Red." In the midst of long talks, walks, and swimming, Warren took him to meet a neighbor, another aspiring writer, Caroline (at that time she spelled it Carolyn) Gordon. Caroline was a living exhibit of the fantasies that Tate's mother had told him about his Virginia ancestors. Caroline's eccentric, dominating mother was a Meriwether, from the leading landed family in that part of southern Kentucky. The family controlled, and operated in almost baronial style, thousands of acres of fertile Kentucky soil. The main plantation, Merry Mont, still reflected some of the glory of a more prosperous, almost feudal past. The Meriwethers were also known, locally, for their many eccentricities. Indeed, the clan and the place exuded a Faulkner-like element of decay. The matriarch of the clan, Miss Carrie Meriwether, frequently hosted the Tates.

Caroline, after an apprenticeship in journalism, was deeply committed to literature, to being a novelist, but shared with Tate a rebellious trait, a desire to break away from bourgeois values. Following Tate back to New York in the fall of 1924, she soon joined the chaotic life of intellectuals in Greenwich Village. She wanted to be with Tate, was in love with him, and would soon marry him. The Tates always dated their marriage from the fall of 1924, but it is notable that Tate wrote Davidson that they had just married in May 1925, or only four months before the birth of their only child, Nancy.[11]

After leaving Guthrie, Tate moved permanently to New York City (he had visted there in the early summer). He exulted in the new freedom and tolerance, met all the leading literary figures, developed a close friendship with Hart Crane and Malcolm Cowley, tried to survive on small fees for book reviews, and at times gained temporary editorial jobs. What is amazing is how quickly he fit himself to the literary scene. He came with no publications save individual poems and reviews. But his intellectual quickness and his unselfish but demanding interest in the writings of everyone else gained him almost immediate respect. He lived a spartan but bohemian life, both before and after his marriage to Caroline. By the summer of 1925 he gained a regular reviewing commitment at the *New Republic* and had almost enough money to live in New York City. But he became increasingly weary of the big city, resentful of the false values that reigned there (who you knew, not quality, assured you access to publishers), and was anxious to have the peace and quiet needed to get more writing completed. Intellectually, his letters reveal much confusion. He lived an exciting life in the city, seemed to enjoy drinking bouts (during prohibition), absorbed and generally accepted the critique of a capitalist society mouthed by leftist friends, but was not ready to capitulate to a stereotypical Marxist solution. And even in Bohemia he kept intact his image as a very civil, polite, Virginia gentleman. He came dressed in a suit and with a cane to his first party in Greenwich Village. But his self-conscious identity as a southerner led to no overt defense of the South. In fact, at first, just the opposite—he clearly saw himself as an exile from the provincial, philistine, and hypocritical South of Eddie Mims, a South that had rejected Tate.

If not committed to the South, Tate certainly sacrificed a great deal to the cause of Southern literature. To the despair of Caroline, Tate offered his New York apartment to any and all writers, and particularly to what she soon referred to as all those "Vanderbilt poets." Their various apartments became hotels, way stations for anyone from back home or, for that matter, anyone who needed a refuge. Both in 1925 and then in 1927 after they moved back into the city, former Fugitives, like Warren, or later Agrarians, such as Andrew Lytle, often stayed at the Tates' for weeks or even longer. Also, a loyal Tate became, in effect, the unpaid literary agent of all his former Nashville friends, happily finding them publishers or placing articles for anyone who asked.[12]

Often broke, short on food, the Tates barely survived. Caroline's mother came at the birth of Nancy and, horrified at the primitive and, to her, barbarian mode of life, took the infant back to Kentucky and kept her for the next two years. Caroline, too weak to fight back, lamented that she had her daughter to herself only one day. But the daugher's absence allowed a great experiment. The Tates moved to a farm home in the Berkshires before the winter of 1925–26, paying $8 a month rent. They were usually broke but stayed until the spring of 1927. For a period, Hart Crane moved in to help pay for the needed food. In the winter, isolated, they nearly went mad with cabin fever, and Crane eventually stopped speaking to Tate. In that mad, memorable year, dozens of other friends came by for endless conversation and drinking parties. Caroline could only temporarily escape the unceasing cooking and caring that kept her from her own writing. She also earned money by typing for British novelist Ford Madox Ford, who for long intervals stayed at the farm. She loved rural life and lovingly planted a garden in the summer of 1926. Tate, the later Agrarian, preferred dishwashing to hoeing and never in his life understood anything about farming or had any proclivities for it. But, however blind he was to rural realities, it was during this interlude that Tate found the most compelling cause, and thus the clearest self-image, so far in his confused and rambling life. He embraced, not the South of the present, but an imaginary South of a pre–Civil War era, a South that he knew only obliquely from images of Pleasant Hill or Merry Mont.

For Tate, Mims's *Advancing South* was probably a greater challenge to his identity than the Scopes Trial. He had to refute Mims, and with him all the New South crowd. Tate's original response to Mims's book was quite mild. He believed Mims never said anything quite wrong, "just a little vulgar and, because he is dishonest, stupid." But on a more careful reading, he pronounced it "probably the worst book ever written on any subject." Mims, "as a defender of culture," is "its greatest enemy." Almost immediately Tate began work on an essay on fundamentalism and the Scopes Trial. He planned to define the rights of both science and religion, but with the advantage given to religion. Scientists tell us nothing about reality and have no right to deny any ontology. Yet the church had no right to arbitrate scientific issues. Tate never completed such an essay, although his theme informed at least two critical essays and closely tied his outlook on science to that of Ransom's.[13]

By 1926, Tate was a firm disciple of T. S. Eliot, a young atheist seeking redemption and believable absolutes. He was also a social critic, with as radical a critique of modern bourgeois society as any Marxist, but he already wanted a reactionary rather than a liberal or socialist solution to all the problems. By December 1926, after several digs at southern provincialism in his essays and reviews, he used a critique of Davidson's *Tall Men* gratuitously to concede that southerners were better men than the Yankees. He was beginning to assess his own heritage. Perhaps more accurately, as he became a parent and began to recapitulate his own childhood, he began to create for himself an authentic southern heritage. Three months later, he had completed his conversion and, in a sense, had found his temporary substitute for the church and its absolutes that he always celebrated but, typical of moderns, could not really believe in. On 1 March 1927, he wrote Davidson: "I've attacked the South for the last time, except in so far as it may be necessary to point out that the chief defect the Old South had was that in it which produced, through whatever cause, the New South." This made clear his continued contempt for much in the contemporary South, where decay was so deep, so organic, that almost no southerner could appreciate pure southern poetry (he referred primarily to his own). He pointed out the need for a publishing outlet for true southern literature, as distinct from the New South junk, such as local color or, better, colored localism, continuously fed to the Yankee market.[14]

Tate's letter elicited a fervent response from Davidson, but with less than a full grasp of Tate's ideological perspective or his apocalyptic views about the present. Davidson, endorsing Tate's condemnation of the New South movement, said that on this issue he could hardly trust himself to write. He was "very much stirred up," but targeted his anger at Sinclair Lewis's *Elmer Gantry,* a portrait of a cad by a cad. Such a visceral reaction all but missed Tate's point, for Tate also found plenty of Elmer Gantrys in the modern South. Davidson hoped a sense of humor and balance would prevent him from becoming a Bourbon in the extreme. A week later, Tate proposed that Davidson and Ransom join him in writing a book of prose essays in defense of the South—the first specific suggestion for what became *I'll Take My Stand*. This time Davidson responded with passion: "I'll join in and go the limit." He was "willing to write on almost anything" after a month to catch up on his work. Ransom's response was a bit more subdued. He had a hard time descending from the philosophical heights. He expressed delight, but he had little time to think about it. He did not foresee a book on southern literature, for too little existed to clarify a principle. Thus, the authors should go right to the principle and point out that an esthetic life was better lived in the Old South than written about. He noted that he had just completed an article to make this point.[15]

Just after his proposal for a symposium, a financially desperate Tate signed a publisher's contract to write a biography of Stonewall Jackson. He later cited purely financial reasons, since such a task seemed to war against his commitment to a southern symposium. In fact, his work on this hastily written, deliberately partisan book did more than anything else to solidify his newfound southern loyalties. He and Caroline spent part of the summer of 1927 visiting battlefield sites and ancestral homes in Virginia. Soon intensely involved in Jackson's career, deeply committed to the Confederate cause, and pulled back into the mystique of his own Virginia ancestors, Tate ended the book as a latter-day Confederate. He so internalized the culture of the Old South that before long he challenged a critic to a duel, but promised Davidson that he would not shoot the scoundrel. The well-written, partisan biography sold well. For the first time ever, Tate was able to save some money. Agreeing to do the biography helped secure a publisher's contract for his first volume of poems, and the strong reviews for both books helped him win a Guggenheim fellowship in 1928. This would fund a year's study in France. Before he and Caroline left for Europe, he signed a new contract for a biography of Jefferson Davis. He had scant time to think about the symposium and seems to have forgotten the whole idea.[16]

Ransom did have the time. The new article he referred to in his March 1927 letter to Tate turned out to be his opening salvo in a defense of the South and his first answer to Mims's book. He first sent his new article to the *Nation*. It rejected it. He had first called it "Pioneering on Principle." Next he sent it to the *Sewanee Review*, then edited by a later protagonist of the Agrarians, William Knicker-bocker. His submission title, "Reconstructed but Unregenerate," seemed too strong for the *Review.* Thus, on request, Ransom changed it to "The South—Old or New," and it appeared in April 1928. Sub-sequently he revised the same article for *Harper's Weekly* and pub-lished it in June 1929 as "The South Defends Its Heritage." Finally he revived his earlier title, considerably expanded many of the ar-guments, and published it as his essay in *I'll Take My Stand.* More than any other single article, this essay anticipated the manifesto that Ransom wrote as an introduction for *I'll Take My Stand,* and which alone gave an early semblance of unity to what people would soon call Agrarianism.

In his original essay, Ransom noted the widely accepted view that the South was now a hundred percent American, forward look-ing, in the process of being modernized and industrialized (the view of Mims). He doubted this was so and hoped it was not. The South should show how to master industrialization, not capitulate to it. He believed Southern traditions opposed industrialism, for the origi-nal South was rooted in what Ransom, quite confusingly, called "European principles." Of course, early Englishmen had pioneered, but that was well in the past. Since then, Englishmen had lived on their establishments, enjoying wonderfully stable customs and insti-tutions in law, literature, and, above all, material conditions. This led to appropriate ways of making a living along lines of least re-sistance, and easy and routine lives within a tradition that allowed security, leisure, and intellectual freedom. Conservatives all, these Englishmen put energy into the life of the mind, renouncing prac-tical ambition and the materialistic dreams of youth. Thus, Ran-som had arrived at his own model of the good life—a society aristo-cratic in its social relations and political leadership, traditional in its culture, and orthodox in its religion. Such themes seemed, at best, to fit only the antique gentry in twentieth-century Britain. But Ransom's idealization of such a culture echoed philosophers George Santayana and Benedetto Croce, whom he had been reading.

Opposite to such "European principles" were the pioneering val-ues dominant in most of modern America, save among the rem-nants of the old culture still holding out in the South. Ransom viewed the pioneering style of life as ultimately absurd, for it involved a perennial fight against nature. Men struggled to subdue it, and, armed by applied science, they had in part wrested it to their mold through modern industrial techniques. Ambition, competition, avarice, and an ultimate impiety marked the masculine form of this struggle against nature. The feminine aspect was service, a perennial do-goodism that led to missionary efforts to change and uplift other benighted people. Such pioneering, ever more hurried and frantic, could never lead to happiness, for nature would eventually wear down even Yankees. Submission, respect was far wiser, and such respect found an outlet in religion and art. Ransom wanted the South to adhere to the older established ideals, to resist any addiction to work, reform, and material gain, and to keep leisure as a part of all work and play. In themes later emphasized by Donald Davidson, he celebrated the folk arts of the older South—dress, conversation, manners, cuisine, the hunt, politics, oratory, the pulpit—all arts of living, and not of show or escape, and arts enjoyed by all classes. Such a culture lingered on in other regions, such as New England, but such a "peace with nature" was most deeply entrenched in the still largely rural and agricultural South (he did not yet use the label Agrarian).

But Ransom wanted to avoid a nostalgic retreat into the past. The Civil War had done great material damage to the South, or to the foundations of its culture. The South, beset by poverty, now needed some pioneering to restore its economy, and short of such economic gains offered a weak counterpoint to industrialism. The South needed to do more than sing pitiful songs about the old order. It had only shabby equipment for a good life. When one can hardly live, materially, no art of living is possible. Too many broken-down Southerners did not labor at all. Now the industrialists were holding out their lures, and the urban South had already capitulated. Not so the farmers and villagers. Ransom's final question—how could this traditional, established, European South resist the new external enemies and thus preserve its ancient heritage and integrity? How could it develop its resources without making the development an end in itself? He provided no answers.[17]

Although committed to a symposium on the South as early as the spring of 1927, neither Ransom, Davidson, nor Tate worked to get it under way. They talked about it, began recruiting possible al-

Robert Penn Warren and his first wife, Cinina Brescia (Photo by
Associated Press)

lies, but were too diverted by other commitments. By the fall of 1927, Ransom was full of the new cause. He proclaimed "Our cause" as the Old South. He told Tate he now liked his own people. They were better than the Yankees and were gaining self-confidence as Southerners, not as applicants for the club up in New York City. He took heart in the fact that Tate, a refugee, remained so loyal to his home. Ransom began celebrating even the physical beauty of the South and saw that "our fight is for survival, and it's got to be waged not so much against the Yankees as against the exponents of a New South."[18]

In September 1928, Allen and Caroline Tate moved to Europe for his Guggenheim year. For two months they stayed in London. Tate met every important literary figure but rejoiced most in getting to know his hero, T. S. Eliot. Then, in Paris for the winter, they met all the American literary expatriates or visitors. They were able to live free in Ford Madox Ford's apartment. They mixed all the social opportunities with desperate bouts of writing. Tate admired — and partied a bit — with Ernest Hemingway, somewhat reluctantly paid his obligatory respects to Gertrude Stein (he thought she was a fake), formed a deep friendship with a true soul mate, John Peale Bishop, and in spite of the usual chaos of guests and frequent moves, finally completed his Jeff Davis biography.[19]

The book exuded Tate's newfound loyalty to southern independence. He painted in lurid colors the Yankee determination to subdue the South, but he admitted that the South was a class society, and that the larger planters had soon thirsted for their own empire. But they still supported "Conservative Fundamentalist Christianity" and a "civilization based on Agrarian, class rule, in the European sense." Unlike Ransom, Tate saw the North as increasingly Europeanized, for he identified industrialism with Europe, but admitted that the South aped an older Europe, in fact was now closer to the older European model than Europe itself. Because of his emotional commitment to a Southern victory, his portrait of Davis was ambivalent. In personal ways, Davis was almost a saint, the greatest statesman that America ever produced. But by that very fact he was an inept politician and Tate all but blamed him for southern defeat. "God alone" could forgive him his fatal loyalty to General Braxton

Bragg or any number of other fatal blunders that revealed the flaw of any saint as politician.[20]

While in Europe, Tate wrote his first major philosophical essay, one that directly influenced *I'll Take My Stand*. Tate and Ransom were very much aware of what some called the New Humanism, a loosely unified philosophical and critical movement led by Irving Babbitt and Paul Elmer More at Harvard. The classical values of these humanists seemed very close, if not identical, to the developing views of Tate and Ransom. Feeling a bit threatened, Tate wanted to draw enough distinctions to separate his views from such "allies" in the great cause of cultural reaction. He responded avidly to a suggestion from T. S. Eliot that he write an article on the New Humanists for publication in Eliot's journal, the *Criterion*. Tate put more effort into this article than any he had ever written. The results drew plaudits from Eliot and rave reviews from Ransom. For the first time, Tate felt that he was able to make a philosophical contribution to what he was already, at times, referring to as an agrarian position (he seems to have been the first to adopt this label).

Tate was not always fair to Babbitt and More. He was given to overkill. He accepted the humanist critique of modernity but argued that this was not enough. Both Babbitt and More correctly affirmed human uniqueness and a world of value not accessible to the tools of science. But they offered no philosophical support for their view. They were flaccid modernists after all, for they defended no specific values, no specific traditions, and never advanced any method of vindicating the values that people affirm. Tate wanted to back up a humanistic philosophy with objective criteria, and beyond that with either ontological foundations or the authority of a supernatural religion. Babbitt finessed these issues completely, supporting a humanist position anchored only by classical knowledge and his personal affirmation. More claimed religious support, but on investigation Tate found his religion exceedingly eclectic and ecumenical, at no point tied to specific dogmas. His was the snare either of a religion in general or a religion tied ultimately to subjective authority. More affirmed an all-too-typical modern religion of sincerity and good feelings. Equally subjective was his morality and even his literary judgments. Tate craved a specific, historical religion, one that claimed objective authority for its dogmas. Without that, he argued, the New Humanists were still closet naturalists. He rejected any humanism that floated in the abstract air, tied to no particular tradition, place, and god.[21]

Ransom seemed to agree with Tate. This is odd, for the philosophical position defended by More seemed very close to that of Ransom, who eventually accepted a naturalism broad enough to encompass human culture and human values. But in 1929 he was at work on his eccentric book, *God Without Thunder*. Not only was he immersed in religious issues, but by now he made religion the fundamental issue in defending the Old South. He thus argued with Tate that religion was the only effective defense against "Progress, & a very vicious economic system, against empire and against socialism, or any other political foolishness." Upon religion depended the security and enjoyment of life. The beginning of wisdom was fear of the Lord, the end love of the Lord. But, in a qualification that symbolized the enormous gulf that always separated him from Tate, he added: "Substitute nature for the Lord and he won't feel aggrieved." What united him and Tate was a common, developing repugnance at Christian liberalism and modernism. By now, Ransom had found an idealized religion, that which reflected a profound piety before an inscrutable nature, in the Old Testament, and saw the beginning degeneration of such a pious and mythic religion in the New Testament, for in the idea of the incarnation, in the man Jesus who, by his disciples, was elevated into the status of a god, Ransom saw the beginnings of an indulgent or humanist religion. God was always on the way to domestication, to being a nice servant of humans. The end was modernist Christianity, with God reduced to the spirit of love or the spirit of science or the spirit of Rotary, and religion a secular crutch as people became gods.[22]

Even as Ransom helped collect the essays for *I'll Take My Stand*, he was able to complete publication of his very self-revealing book — *God Without Thunder: An Unorthodox Defense of Orthodoxy*. Revealingly, he dedicated the book to his father. In a sense he remained, or wanted to remain, a good Methodist. That was impossible. It was a book on gods, one in which Ransom bared his taste in gods. He liked the old style, or gods of thunder, gods that invited fear and trembling, that created both good and evil. He went back to the Old Testament and in arguments very close to those of mod-

ern neoorthodox theologians, from Kierkegaard to Barth, castigated
those soft, sentimental, indulgent gods of modernity, those gods
without thunder. He placed himself squarely on the side of anthro-
pomorphic and supernatural gods, those who were rooted in natural wonder and manifested in compelling stories or myths. Such
gods do not mesh with scientific intelligence, even stand as an affront to it. In a rather eccentric analysis, he identified such gods
with the ancient Orient and traced the Western or Greek perver-
sions of such a tradition. Even the Christ, the Logos concept of
Western theology, was a perversion, and in the abstractions of early
Greek theology he found, quite suggestively, the origins of the later
scientific, materialistic outlook that produced a modern industrial
society. But the flavor of the old gods lingered in the superstitions
and myths of the Middle Ages, and lingered still in southern fundamentalism. His demotion of Jesus made him, technically, a uni-
tarian. But the modern liberal religion of a Kirkland or a Mims was
a product of essentially impious men, of men who denied evil, de-
fied fate, and foolishly claimed human omnipotence. An industrial,
artificial, consumer culture was only one result.

Despite Ransom's cleverness, *God Without Thunder* leaves a reader
more perplexed than persuaded. One of similar taste may well applaud Ransom's god. His choice might even be quite consistent
with an openness to poetry or even to a stable and humane social
order. On this one can argue. But one has no sense that Ransom,
personally, stood in fear and trembling before any god. The book
was artful social criticism, not religious confession. If such gods
were beyond his own vital belief, then Ransom could not in good
faith recommend them to the peasants.[23]

Donald Davidson never soared quite so high into the philosophical and theological ether as Ransom and Tate. But he knew ten
times as much about the South, whether old or new. His work with
the book page of the *Tennessean* gave him an amazingly detailed
knowledge of literary and other artistic activity in the South. He
also read, and reviewed, many books on southern history and society. At times, he already revealed a fascination with folk culture
and with regional differences. The broader philosophical theories
of Tate and Ransom generally persuaded him, but he did little to
amplify their antimodernist perspective. Notably, in these years he

professed no personal interest in theology and never attended or joined a church. At times he even reflected a mild anticlericalism. He tried to be more scholarly and more balanced than Tate and Ransom in what he published about the South. He sent various reference books to Tate in an effort to get him to make his biography of Jackson thoroughly scholarly but was not persuaded that Tate passed the test. In the early planning of the projected symposium, Davidson seemed willing to recruit "liberals" or "progressives" so long as they offered possible solutions to southern problems. He conceived of a book focused on specific problems and directed at practical solutions. He even considered Mims as a possible contributor. Typically, he kept addressing the practical issue of making a new point of view known and winning converts for what he hoped would be an active political crusade. By early 1929 he wrote Tate about the prospects for a new southern magazine. By then, he, Ransom, and John Wade (a new English professor at Vanderbilt) were at work on the projected symposium, although, one feels, in a somewhat desultory way. Davidson even asked Tate if he would contribute, a somewhat strange invitation since Tate had originally proposed the volume. Perhaps, as Davidson already realized, such a volume would require a lot of editorial work, and that he would probably have to do most of it himself. Ransom was an idea man, not a worker, and Tate was in France.[24]

By July 1929, Davidson could write Tate that he was now agitating for the new symposium, with partial and hesitant encouragement from Ransom. From a general symposium, open to all shades of opinion, he had now decided on a partisan book, one reflecting the philosophy of the three of them. Eventually, Ransom persuaded Davidson that it should also be a book addressed to broad philosophical issues, postponing until later any practical programs. In any case, the contributors would have to be native southerners of "our mind" and with vigorous ideas. Davidson had by then an outline of topics and had already written Doubleday about a possible contract. He was stirred to such action by news of a proposed symposium to be edited by Howard Mumford Jones and to be dominated by the North Carolina progressives, such as Howard Odum. The progressives might capture the field, win over public opinion, and violate southern traditions by their treatment of the Negro is-

sue, already a more critical concern to Davidson than the philosophical heresies that bothered Tate. Again, Davidson asked Tate not
only to contribute but to indicate the topic of his essay.[25]

This letter, and other correspondence from Ransom, provoked
a detailed response from Tate. Significantly, he first sent his new proposals to Warren, who was still at Oxford. This amounted to an
early effort to recruit him for the book. Tate, a temporary exile
from the South, waxed eloquent in his sweeping proposal. Why not
a society or academy of "Southern positive reactionaries," with eventually up to fifteen active members? Why not a philosophical con-
stitution or a creed, setting forth a complete social, philosophical
literary, economic, and religious system, a system tied to a southern heritage, though based not on southern performance but the
perfection of an ideal. He believed the actual Old South was not
so good a prototype as the historical and religious scheme of an
older Europe, but it was their particular heritage and their cause.
His academy, although not to be secret, was to plot in secret, and
thus Tate seemed to have in mind a small revolutionary cadre, like
a Communist Party cell. After the academy would come organized
publications, such as a newspaper, a weekly, and a quarterly. The
advantage of this approach was that of any extreme, cohesive movement. It would show up the unorganized muddle of liberals and progressives. Even to assert principles (no more might be possible), the
group had to be disciplined. To fight centralization, they had to be
centralized, and for this reason had to reject one aspect of the southern and Jeffersonian tradition. He would prefer the academy first,
then the projected symposium. But time allowed no such delay,
since he wanted only people open to the disciplined academy to contribute essays. He listed possible contributors, though he showed
such an involvement with the religious issue that no imaginable contributor would have ever satisfied him; but at this time he himself
planned to write on the New Humanism.[26]

With Tate not only in, but pushing way ahead of a more cautious
Davidson and a still tentative Ransom, the publication of what
would become *I'll Take My Stand* was almost assured. In just a year,
largely through the work of Davidson, the book would be ready for
the publisher. Its publication launched a new stage in the development of Southern Agrarianism.

III.

The Book

Most people identify Southern Agrarianism completely with one book, *I'll Take My Stand*. This is a mistake. The book was, at best, only a prelude to an organized agrarian movement. Even in volume its twelve essays made up no more than a sixth of the important agrarian essays eventually composed by its twelve contributors. It also lacked the focus, and the practical programs, that came later. Yet, in American literary history, and in the history of broad cultural criticism, it remains a landmark book, still alive, still in print, and still read by varied and appreciative audiences. Obviously, as Tate, Ransom, and Davidson began soliciting contributors in the hot summer of 1929, they had no intimation of such fame. They simply wondered if they could possibly complete a book that would appeal to a publisher.

By then, the problem was getting enough people to write on what seemed to be obligatory subjects. They needed essays on southern economics, education, history, literature, politics, religion, and tradition, plus some attention to the Negro problem and, if possible, the status of women (they discussed various women contributors but gave up the recruitment effort, one feels, without deep regrets). Tate had only two names to suggest as extra contributors—John Gould Fletcher and his closest friend, Robert Penn Warren.

Fletcher had long since volunteered. After visiting the Fugitives while in the United States in 1927, and hearing firsthand of tentative plans for a symposium, he had expressed his strong desire to be part of any such effort. Fletcher in 1927 was an exiled poet living in England. He was a son of a wealthy Little Rock family, pushed by family expectations to Harvard. By then a sensitive, unhappy misfit, he fled to Europe before he graduated. There he gained a reputation for poetic experimentation in a movement called Imagism (typified by Amy Lowell's work, this poetry turned away from any coherent cognitive content). By 1928, Fletcher had begun moving back toward his Arkansas roots, emotionally but not yet in fact, and had begun to repudiate his earlier literary experimentation. In the late twenties his philosophical outlook seemed very close to that of Tate's — a positive reaction. In letters to Davidson he revealed his anger at a corrupted and vulgar modern age. But Tate, from his earlier confusions, was moving toward a coherent philosophical stand. Unfortunately, a mentally beset Fletcher was moving toward even greater confusion, to a horrible erosion of ego, and thus toward periodic mental breakdowns and erratic, unpredictable crusades. He had great talent, and at his best was brilliant, genial, engaging, but he was always a risk in ideological warfare, as the other Agrarians would eventually find out. When formally asked to contribute in early 1930, Fletcher asked to do the essay on education. He found a temporary meaning for his life in joining with the Agrarians and was the first to submit a completed essay.[1]

Tate had always assumed Robert Penn Warren would join the pro-South movement. He had unlimited admiration for Red, both personally and for his unlimited literary skills. As Tate remembered it, he first met Warren in 1923 when the tall, thin, red-haired Vanderbilt student walked into his dorm room and shared with him a sophomoric (he was a sophomore) poem on hell. Briefly they would be roommates before Tate left Nashville. In the next academic year, Warren fell into a deep depression, for reasons never completely clear. The son of a banker in little Guthrie, Kentucky, with a secure childhood and supportive parents, Warren nonetheless suffered a series of blows to his personal ego. An injury to an eye blocked his planned application to the Naval Academy. At Vanderbilt he plunged, perhaps too deeply, into the intellectual tensions of the English department and the Fugitive group. His bad eye worsened and he feared blindness. Too deep in depression to function effectively, he attempted suicide and then fled back home to Guthrie. Tate joined him, and all the people back at Vanderbilt tried to be supportive. Most would visit him in Guthrie. By the fall of 1924 he was able to resume his studies and to graduate in the spring of 1925. A brilliant undergraduate record gained him a fellowship at Berkeley.

Except for his continued friendship with Tate, Warren more or less left the Vanderbilt circle. He did not like Berkeley or find graduate work half so challenging as the Fugitive seminars. He was, at times, a bit wild and rebellious. He transferred to Yale in 1927. On the way East, and on at least two other occasions, he spent long periods with the Tates and must have heard all about the early plans for a symposium on the South. In 1928 he won a Rhodes scholarship and moved to Oxford. But, if anything, distance increased his affection for his old Fugitive friends and, aided by Tate, he was able to get a contract for his first book, a biography of John Brown (1929), which kept before him the problem of slavery and of the South. Thus, when Davidson and Tate begged him to do the essay on the Negro for the symposium, Warren accepted. He was busy, late in finishing it, and seemed diffident, even casual, about the product.[2]

What was not clear was how much Warren was committed to the agrarian cause. He was fascinated with the South or, better put, with all the various Souths. He had home loyalties and would almost always turn to these as subjects for his later novels. Much more acutely than any other Agrarian, he attended to the nuanced particulars of life in the South. And, as a writer, he easily identified with many of the philosophical themes developed by Ransom and Tate. Yet he never capitulated to any ideology or committed himself unreservedly to the Southern cause. And none of his essays, in *I'll Take My Stand* or later, spoke directly to the philosophical issues. He preferred to do literary criticism, or to describe various points of view, as a somewhat detached observer, whimsical and sympathetic. At the Fugitive reunion at Vanderbilt in 1956, Warren remembered that the agrarian cause appealed to him because he was young, away from home, and sentimentally attached to a familiar way of life. He was willing to affirm his roots, not as a thought-out philosophy but as an intuitive response. At Oxford, he talked often with

MASQUERADEI

Cartoon of Davidson, Tate, and Ransom on cover of Vanderbilt humor magazine, 1933

students who hated the dehumanizing effects of machines and factories. Like most Southerners, he had absorbed heroic stories of the Civil War. He saw his participation as a way to use a vision of a simple past age and place as a means of protest against the disintegration and dehumanization of his age. The past was a proper rebuke to the present, and he thus defined his effort largely in historical terms. The drama of the past that corrects is the ever-recurrent drama of our own struggles to be human.[3]

Much more passionately involved was Andrew Lytle, one of Warren's fellow students at Vanderbilt. At first, no one seemed to think of Lytle, from an old, established family of nearby Murfreesboro, as a contributor. But he was an active worker in the cause at least from 1928 on. After getting his degree in English at Vanderbilt in 1925, Lytle worked for his father for a year and then moved to Yale University in 1926 to study playwriting and drama under George Pierce Baker. While at Yale in 1927, he came over to New York City to spend time with the Tates (he was another one of those Vanderbilt poets, but a sweet one that Caroline soon adored). Even then, Tate hoped Lytle could help the new southern cause by writing appropriate plays but at the time did not feel he had the quality of mind of a Warren. Lytle, who never completed a new play he had tried to write as part of his workshop at Yale, took some temporary acting jobs in New York City, but finally gave up on a career in the theatre by 1929. He could do this because his father needed him to help manage a large plantation, named Cornsilk, outside Guntersville, Alabama. Also in 1929 he signed the contract for his first book, a biography of Nathan Bedford Forrest, thus following the pattern set by Tate and Warren. By then, still single and full of energy, he seemed always on the move, from Murfreesboro to Cornsilk to the family cabin at Monteagle or trips to New York City. Interspersed were visits to his friends in Nashville. He and his father made the Alabama farm into a type of retreat for ex-Fugitives or future Agrarians. Just before leaving for Europe in 1928, the Tates joined others of the future agrarian brethren at Cornsilk in a typical gathering. Later the farm became a favorite retreat for the Tates, as did Andrew's cabin at Monteagle. The appealing name of the Lytle plantation also set a precedent—whenever the Agrarians later bought land, they always invented appealing names for their farms.[4]

Lytle was never a philosopher in the sense of Ransom, and was much more an equalitarian Jeffersonian than an aristocrat, but he had as visceral and deep a commitment to the South and to its ordinary yeomen as did Davidson. He also had Davidson's talent for simple, direct, sharp, pungent, eloquent prose, and Warren's ability to describe, in nuanced detail, the life and speech of various, often backwoods, southerners. By 1930, as Ransom and Davidson tried to put the volume of essays together, a helpful Lytle was always available, at times as involved and as busy as either Davidson or Ransom. In a sense, he won a right to contribute and completed "The Hind Tit" on schedule.

Warren and Lytle were young and without established reputations. They were welcome contributors but in a sense had to justify themselves by excellent essays. As the main architects of the volume realized, they had to enlist not just prodigies but some eminent scholars. They wrote to four or five outside journalists or scholars, only to be turned down. Stringfellow Barr of the *Virginia Quarterly Review* at first expressed a desire to participate but later wanted such modifications in the statement of principles that Davidson decided to drop him. This made more crucial the cooperation of the most distinguished Vanderbilt possibility, Frank Owsley of the History department.

Owsley was, in age, close to Ransom. Born on a Montgomery County, Alabama, farm in 1890, he took his B.A. and M.A. in history at Auburn, before moving on to brilliant but often traumatic graduate work at the University of Chicago. Before completing a dissertation under William E. Dodd, he joined the Vanderbilt history faculty in 1920. He completed the Ph.D. in 1924 and in 1925 published his dissertation, *State Rights in the Confederacy,* a book that very much influenced both Tate and Davidson. In 1927–28, just as the agrarian effort got under way at Vanderbilt, Owsley moved to England on a prized Guggenheim, there completing research for his second book, the very important *King Cotton Diplomacy* (1931). His absence accounts for not only his lack of participation in the early planning, but for the absence of his name on any of the early lists of possible contributors. Although Ransom had joined Owsley on university committees, they apparently had never talked on political or philosophical issues. Thus, it was a pleasant

Caroline Gordon, Allen Tate, and Sally Wood in France, 1932

surprise when Owsley returned, immediately full of enthusiasm for the projected book and pointing out that his loyalty to the South predated that of any of the poets. In fact, his later views would distinguish him from Ransom, in particular, for Owsley was more radical in his economic views, more chauvinistic in his defense of the South, and much more rigid in his support of racial segregation. Since the book had to have a historian, Owsley seemed a perfect contributor. Actually, he was too busy to write a new essay and thus like others, including Ransom, he recycled an older one.[5]

The final two local contributors never had the passionate commitment of Owsley. First was Lyle Lanier, a young, professionally ambitious Vanderbilt psychologist and an expert on the issue of racial differences in intelligence. Lanier became a close friend and an academic ally of Ransom and was much respected by Tate. A "neighbor" from Middle Tennessee and an earlier Vanderbilt graduate, he was an astute critic of the more imperialistic claims of social scientists. In a general way he subscribed to the agrarian cause, brought to the cultural and economic issues a badly needed balance and fairness, and from 1930 to 1937 was always a valued member of what soon everyone referred to as "the brethren," or the eight Nashville Agrarians who met and partied as often as possible.

The other local member was an English department colleague, John Donald Wade, a very loyal native of Marshallville, Georgia. After resigning a position at the University of Georgia over a point of principle, he took a position at Vanderbilt in 1926 (age 34) to help create a new graduate program in American literature. Still unmarried, he almost became a commuting professor; he usually boarded in the Hermitage Hotel during semesters, only to flee back to the family home, and his mother, in Marshallville as soon as he could. He gained the Vanderbilt position because of a pioneer biography (1925) on the Southern humorist, Augustus Baldwin Longstreet, and became an authority on both Southern humor and his beloved Methodist church. Since his work was primarily in biography, his approach to literature was at the opposite pole from the internalist criticism later advocated by Ransom and Tate. Wade would never be an ideologue. A gentle person in love with home and gardens, a loyal booster of his hometown, deeply committed to his state of Georgia, he never quite fit the agrarian harness. But Ran-

Lyle Lanier

som and Tate touched on issues, on familiar traditions, that moved Wade, and for a few years he tried, in his modest way, to help the cause. At times he was envious of the more overt activism of the other authors for, in his own reaction to troubling and confusing events, he was more likely to retreat than to fight. Above all, he defended local village and rural values, those of his people, against urban ones. He would use an already completed biographical sketch as his contribution to *I'll Take My Stand.* In 1934 he returned to the University of Georgia, in part because it brought him nearer to Marshallville. He maintained a very close friendship with Davidson but did not know most of the other brethren well.[6]

Another but ill-fitted Vanderbilt contributor was Henry Blue Kline. He had just completed an M.A. in the English department and had impressed both Davidson and Ransom with his abilities. Apparently, Davidson asked him to submit an essay, but with no assurance that it would qualify for the book. Kline, desperately seeking an academic position, knew a published essay would help his cause (he gained an instructorship at the University of Tennessee in the fall of 1930 but would later move on to a position with the Tennessee Valley Authority). He had trouble with his essay and did not know until the last minute whether Davidson or Ransom would accept it. They did. They made a mistake, for it was not even close to the quality of the other essays. But Kline was agreeable, flattered Davidson with long letters, professed his full conversion to Agrarianism, and gladly made any editorial changes suggested by Davidson. Neither Davidson nor Ransom had the heart to turn him down in the end, and they needed his essay in order to make twelve (eleven would not have sounded right).[7]

All along, Davidson and Ransom had sought a contributor who could address the economic problems of the South, particularly those in agriculture. They considered several possibilities before turning to a former colleague, Herman Clarence Nixon. Until 1928 he had been a member of the History department at Vanderbilt, but then had moved to Tulane. Apparently he knew nothing about the proposed symposium before he left Nashville. He knew, but was not close to, the people in the English department. He was born in 1886 at Merrellton, Alabama (near Jacksonville). His father, an aggressive, ambitious country merchant, owned more land than anyone else in Calhoun County. Nixon's background and career was amazingly similar to that of his slightly younger friend, Owsley— each attended Auburn, each there completed an M.A. under the same advisor, and each took a Ph.D. in history under Dodd at the University of Chicago. Nixon served in World War I, then taught briefly in Alabama and at Iowa State University before completing his dissertation and joining his friend Owsley at Vanderbilt in 1925.

For Nixon, the word "Agrarian" stood for the interest of farmers, particularly small farmers. His dissertation, on Iowa populism, permanently oriented his concerns toward the problems of small farmers, while a Christian social gospel oriented him toward the needs of the poor and lowly. Distinctive among social scientists, he always wrote in a pungent and effective way. Nixon had stronger class loyalties than any other of the contributors to *I'll Take My Stand*. The more hierarchical or traditional ideals of Ransom had no appeal for him. He wanted to help the plain folks and to get rid of all forms of special privilege and all types of exploitation. In most respects, he and Owsley agreed on economic issues, including support for land reform, for public ownership of resources and public utilities, and for some type of socialized public health care. But at this time Nixon was unique among the contributors in always including Negroes in his reforms, and in his later willingness, at great personal sacrifice, to join organizations that supported the full equality of blacks.

Davidson helped recruit Nixon for the project. But not without some concern. Was he one of them? Nixon, in most respects, quieted such apprehensions. He was enthusiastic about the book and agreed with most of the proposed principles that would preface it. He wanted to avoid attacks on New South boosters, but only because there was no New South. He felt no need to whip industrialism, for it was already discredited. Even in early 1930 he anticipated the coming great depression. He felt comfortable with a celebration of an old, stable, Jeffersonian South, the South of independent yeomen. He soon became a fervent supporter of Franklin D. Roosevelt, along with most of the Agrarians, and at least until 1935 felt that he was fully a part of the group, although at too great a distance to become one of the brethren.[8]

The final contributor to *I'll Take My Stand* fit into a special cate-

Herman C. Nixon (Photo by Walden Fabry)

gory. This was Stark Young. The organizers of the symposium knew that they needed recognized names to attract publishers. They considered southerners who had made good in the North, such as Gerald Johnson (he turned them down and later repudiated their principles). Young's name came up frequently. He was older (almost 50 in 1930), from Mississippi, had already published novels, had written several plays, and had become deeply entrenched in New York literary circles. For a period he had served as drama critic for the *New Republic* (Tate met him in that capacity) and later wrote hundreds of critical essays for several magazines. By 1930 he was arguably the most prominent drama critic in America, and his later Civil War novel, *So Red the Rose,* continues to win critical praise. He knew and was respected by everyone who counted nationally in drama and literature but was personally acquainted with only Tate among the Vanderbilt Agrarians. As soon as Tate returned to America in January 1930 from his stretched-out Guggenheim, Davidson had him contact Young in order to get him to join their project. Young gladly did so, and subsequently offered excellent criticism of some of the other essays, but in no ideological sense did he ever become an Agrarian. He loved the South, wrote lovingly but critically about it, but did not make it a cause in the sense that Ransom and Tate did. He was not offended by the agrarian platform but would do little in his graceful essay to support it. Yet, as expected, his involvement did more than that of anyone else to gain the book critical attention, particularly in New York City.[9]

By June 1930, Davidson began receiving the finished essays. Every contributor came through within a month or two of the deadline, a remarkable and rare achievement for any anthology. Ironically, the most eager of the group, Tate, had the most difficult time with his essay, barely getting it to Davidson in time for submission to the publisher. Once again Tate, while in New York in early 1930, had secured the contract with Harper Brothers. Only Davidson, because of prior talks with Doubleday, held up the final agreement. Harpers even offered a $300 advance.

Early copies of the book reached reviewers by early November 1930. It seemed a publishing success. It received hundreds of reviews, led to dozens of articles, and provoked a half dozen well-publicized debates. Yet, in the deepening depression, it sold relatively few copies (only 2,174 until it went out of print in 1941, with total royalties of only $647.14). In a sense, the book was both a success and a disaster. It had no unity. Each essay had to be understood on its own. Yet soon almost everyone had an image of the book, a usually oversimplified image that best survived if one never read the whole book. And, by all the later comments, it seems likely that very few people read all the essays.[10]

The book, in one essay or another, was about almost everything. The language of most essays was loose, ambiguous, suggestive — typical of polemical discourse. The very looseness and diversity allowed sympathetic readers to find what they valued, critical ones to erect damning stereotypes or caricatures. The only point of reference behind all the confusion was a tantalizing title and the opening set of principles. The background to each of those reveals, not a clear purpose, but only papered-over strains and tensions.

The title dated from January or February 1930, when Ransom and Davidson sent a preliminary prospectus to Tate. Wade suggested the opening phrase, "I'll take my stand." At this point, they mainly wanted to attract publishers, and Tate, with no protest against the perhaps tentative title, submitted it to Harper and Row. From then on, the title gained a life of its own and seemed just what the publisher wanted. Later in the summer it became a divisive source of conflict. The controversy involved only the impressionistic lead, "I'll Take My Stand," and not the descriptive subtitle, "The South and the Agrarian Tradition." By 1928, Ransom often used the word "Agrarian" but not with any precision or careful thought. Typical of the times, he simply substituted agrarian for agriculture, for farmers, or for rural life. It is clear that he did not use it in a strict sense to refer to issues of land tenure or to suggest any program of land reform. It gained this meaning only after 1930. Thus, the subtitle did little more than certify that, traditionally, the South had been largely rural and agricultural.

"I'll take my stand," as everyone was supposed to recognize, came from the song "Dixie." Davidson and Ransom, when they decided early in 1930 to give a strongly political emphasis to their book, apparently hoped this phrase would suggest sectional partisanship. They desired a fighting title, although one with playful and whimsical content. No one objected until June, when Warren wrote Tate

from England about how much he disliked "I'll take my stand." Warren returned to America in July and came to visit the Tates. Tate,
supported by Warren, decided that he also hated the lead title, that
he had to effect a last minute change. He did not like the Confederate or parochial images suggested by the words, thought the emotional associations too strong, and thus felt the title would prejudice
readers against the serious, philosophical themes in the essays. Tate
made this a critical, fighting issue and briefly threatened the publication of the book. He seemed on edge during the spring and summer. He still had not completed his essay and was defensive about
it. He had just moved to a farm near Clarksville, one purchased for
him by his brother Ben. His and Caroline's life was close to a normal, frantic chaos, and Tate seemed close to the breaking point.

Davidson and Ransom refused to change the title. Both liked it.
But they handled Tate very carefully. They noted the late date and
the commitment to the publisher but did not offer any elaborate rationalization for the words. Owsley and Lanier joined in accepting,
if not endorsing, the title. As late as September, with the book in
press, Tate resumed the battle, enlisted Lytle as well as Warren on
his side, and tried to get Davidson to put it to a vote of the twelve
authors. Davidson dared not do this and realized that Tate's disciples had no acceptable alternative. Tate wanted to entitle the book
"Tracts Against Communism," a misleading theme endorsed by few
others except Lytle, although to Tate it expressed the strongest argument of the book—that industrialism and communism shared the
same social values, and the book was against these values. For a
few weeks several authors, including even Kline, tossed about possible titles, but none gained broad support. In a last-minute gesture,
however, Ransom and Davidson conceded to Tate the right to insert
a footnote, at the beginning of his essay, taking exception to the
title. This was the only hint of discord in the whole book. In his
note Tate argued that the title suggested exclusiveness instead of the
benefits of a southern emphasis. The South in this case provided
a man-made and imperfect home for the same human spirit that
had lived well in other times and places. Tate saw the Old South
as only one exemplification of a traditional, religious society, and
in many ways a flawed exemplification. He wanted to emphasize,
not the historical South, but certain religious values that found

lodgement in that South. No other contributor shared this particular view. Warren, it is clear from his correspondence, disliked the partisan, politically-loaded implications of the title. He wanted no part of a new Confederacy. [11]

The conflict over a new title probably had one unexpected and unnoticed consequence. It kept Warren's essay in the book. Warren completed his essay just before returning to the States. He accepted the assignment, at Tate's urging, only in March 1930, when Davidson had written: "It's Up To You, Red, to prove that Negroes are country folks . . . 'born and bred in a briar-patch.'" Warren used the briar-patch imagery for his title, but wrote as fair and balanced an essay as he could, and without much effort to adhere to the opening manifesto. He told Tate he assumed it, but in fact did not take it very seriously and never agreed with all of it philosophically. His essay horrified Davidson, who, in alarm, wrote Tate that the essay was not related to the main themes, treated the Negro problem in general terms, with "progressive" implications, and seemed infected by "latter-day sociology." In short, it did not adhere to Southern racial norms and might offend the very Southerners they wanted to enlist in the agrarian cause. In horror, he exclaimed that it did "not sound like him. What is he after?" In fact, he doubted that "Red actually wrote this essay!" He believed it inappropriate for the book, and, after reading it, Owsley fully supported him in this judgment. In this one case, Davidson decided to use his editorial responsibility and reject the essay in order to protect the larger project. He asked Ransom and Lytle to read it, but temporarily held it out of the book. [12]

Tate went to bat for his protégé and friend. He found "Red's essay" to be "very good," and voted to keep it. Warren was right—poor blacks and whites had to end their feud, work together, and find their salvation on the land. Tate admitted, however, that the essay sounded too sociological at points, and invited Davidson to do as Warren had suggested—edit it wherever he wanted. He also conceded a small point of form—Davidson could delete Warren's use of *Mrs.* in reference to a Negro woman. Defeated on the title, itchy for more ideological skirmishes, Tate had to be appeased. Thus, after several small editorial changes, Davidson reluctantly allowed Warren's essay to remain in the book.

The presence of this essay thus early revealed the one time bomb lurking beneath the seeming consensus in *I'll Take My Stand*—race. Warren was sympathetic, generous toward blacks, in favor of their complete equality in a context of social separation. He took Booker T. Washington's arguments and diverted them from industrial progress to agricultural achievements. Such generosity, such goodwill, hinted at treason to the two die-hard defenders of segregation and second-class citizenship—Davidson and Owsley. Although still accepting of conventional social patterns, Warren, Ransom, Tate, and Fletcher did not want to identify Agrarianism with the racial issue. By all indications this was true of Kline and Young. Nixon already wanted to fight openly for Negro equality and for integration. Thus, only so long as the issue it raised remained offstage, separate from an agrarian agenda, could the authors maintain even the fiction of ideological or programmatic unity.[13]

The testimony to unity had to come in the opening set of principles, for the essays were otherwise too diverse, with four already written for other purposes. The idea of a manifesto went back to a letter from Tate in August 1929. He wanted a tight, disciplined movement, modeled on the early Jesuits or on contemporary Communists. Thus, a common manifesto would serve as a test of allegiance and also relieve individuals of any responsibility for what other essayists might write about issues not touched upon in their central platform. Each contributor had to affirm core values but would then be free to write as he wished. In December 1929, Davidson reported that he, Ransom, and Lytle were at work on a credo or manifesto, in the form of a series of articles. Each of them was to write, and submit, his own version of principles. Ransom completed his first; the other two found them acceptable and, except for minor revisions, had no direct role in the outcome. This meant that Ransom almost alone shaped the philosophical position of the book. And, as he warmed to the task, it was clear that he would simply formalize arguments that he had already developed in his article on "The South Old and New" in 1928. By early 1930 he had his manifesto in the form of seventeen articles, or what he desired as a church-like creed or confession for all Agrarians.[14]

In most respects, the seventeen articles paralleled the manifesto published in *I'll Take My Stand*." It would be redundant to summarize the articles here. But they did not include one important theme in the later manifesto—the alleged identity of industrialism and communism—and they included some positions left out later. Three articles, for example, committed the Agrarians to political programs to achieve agrarian goals, including support for consumer boycotts, direct aid to farmers, direct opposition to the Republican Party (the party of industrialism), and even held out the possibility of a new agrarian political party if they could not capture or control the Democratic Party. The article form invited endless amendments and new articles. Tate submitted three. He wanted to take a literary stand—against romanticism and local color—and to stress allegiances with other antimodernist movements but at the same time to use the South as a concrete example of human fulfillment and as a way of pointing to the limitations of the generalized, unanchored platform of the New Humanists.[15]

By February 1930, with the crucial decision to push quickly on to publication, Ransom decided to discard the numbered articles. They invited endless problems. Also, since by then he and the local participants decided on a more generalized appeal, directed not only at southerners but at other like-minded opponents of industrialism, they decided to postpone any detailed practical suggestions. Thus, Ransom recast the articles as the coherent introduction that later appeared in *I'll Take My Stand*. Notably, he then added an indictment of industrialism as inevitably leading to communism but, at Tate's suggestion, did not directly attack socialism (many of Tate's valued friends had a sentimental attachment to socialism). All the participants at least went along with the revised manifesto. Perhaps only Davidson and Ransom were in full agreement with it. Tate noted his reservations about the title, Wade was not happy with the back-to-the-land emphasis, Warren did not take it very seriously, Young noted his disinclination to subscribe to any doctrines, Nixon had only a sentimental attachment to it, and so it went. By the time they read the final version, most had already written their essays or submitted retreads (of the twelve essays, eight were composed specifically for the book, but several of these drew directly from earlier publications). It is not clear that the introductory statement influenced any of the essays except for the two by Ransom and Davidson, who did build consistently upon the manifesto. But, despite its minimal role in shaping the essays, the introduction contained the only common glue for the whole. It alone permits detailed analysis of content.[16]

The manifesto was truistic and involved a vacuous comparison. That is, few people could possibly reject the values portrayed in it, and the implied comparisons were vacuous because no other side really existed. What Ransom did here, as in *God Without Thunder,* was to pile on a series of damning descriptions of what he called industrialism or the modern American system. The South had until recently struggled to resist the dangerous virus of industrialism but lately seemed to be increasingly infected by it, with the infection often spread by the advocates of a new South. The contributors to *I'll Take My Stand* wrote in order to help southerners, or other regional minorities in America, resist "industrialism."

What is "industrialism"? Ransom's answer was at best complex, at worst unclear. First of all, it is a mode of economic organization, involving large collections of capital in the form of plants and tools, centralized management, and dependent wage employees. Ransom emphasized that such collectivized production amounted to a "capitalization" of science. The cruel effects of such collectivism afflict those who work; their "hard, fierce, insecure," brutalizing, servile labors alienate them from the ends and purposes of work and deny to them any leisurely or joyful involvement. Workers also faced the threat of redundancy, as machines took over more and more work. In other words, in an industrial society work ceases to be an art, for it is dedicated not to any intrinsic rewards but only to extrinsic products. It contributes only to a deceptive goal—more and more mindless consumption. Ransom, in his most original argument, noted that the logical end of such industrialism was communism. In fact, as he used the terms, industrialism and communism were all but synonymous, for in their desperate response to the evils of industrialism people turned to socialism or communism, to a more complete form of collectivism than that already prefigured in large corporate enterprise.[17]

Ransom wanted much more than a purely economic definition. But, notably, he began with economic realities and saw these as determinate of all else in a society. The only effective way to check industrialism was to change the mode of organizing capital and mobilizing workers. Welfare tinkering, or sentimental religious or

esthetic approaches, only played at the surface. Given an industrialized economy, then all areas of life were affected by it. Authentic religion, which entailed a submission to an inscrutable nature, could
not survive in an industrial society, one in which people processed
nature, converted it into cities, manufactured it into artificial com-
modities. Such a transformed or corrupted nature invited the illusion of power, a loss of any sense of mystery and contingency, and
turned the gods of yore into amiable and superfluous entities. Likewise, the arts could not cohere with industrialism, for they depend
on a right (mythic, religious) attitude toward nature and require
leisure. The arts of living—manners, hospitality, sympathy, romantic love—also yielded before an industrial order, since they are complementary to religion and art. The ravages of industrialism, im-
mune to meliorative reforms, increased through time, because the
system had an internal dynamic, a constant need for more production and more consumption. The modern stimulants for this were
advertising and salesmanship, means of persuading innocent people to want all the new goods made possible by applied science.[18]

The opposite of industrialism is "agrarianism," a word which
Ransom said did not "stand in particular need of definition." But
Ransom tied it down a bit—to a belief that agriculture, pursued
with intelligence and leisure, is the model vocation, approached
by other necessary tasks as much as possible. An agrarian society
makes the culture of the soil the preeminent vocation, one which
has preference in public policy and one that attracts the most people. Beyond the indictment of industrialism, the elliptical celebration of agrarianism, Ransom eschewed specific policies or programs,
although he asked some questions about possible new legislation,
changes in education, and shifts in party allegiance. He ended his
manifesto on a note of hope. If a section, or race, or age is "groan-
ing under industrialism" and is aware that it is an evil dispensation,
it must find a way to throw it off. Unfortunately, he did not pen
the appropriate ending: "Farmers and poets of the world unite."[19]

What is wrong with this manifesto? Nothing at all. It is very persuasive. It is also commonplace. The very same sentiments rever-
berated through almost all the social criticism of the prior hundred
years, and most forcefully in that of Karl Marx. When, subsequently,
both Tate and Ransom occasionally substituted capitalism for in-

dustrialism, one sensed the verbal similarities with the "Communist Manifesto." But some such critique of an overly commercialized, overly centralized, dependency-creating economic order was present in Emerson and other American Transcendentalists, in John Ruskin and other English rustic socialists, in several strains of Roman Catholic criticism, in extreme antimodernist or neo-feudal advocates, in some forms of European corporatism or fascism, even in the social criticism of such a nemesis as John Dewey. Such a generalized critique touches on almost every profound concern of the twentieth century, from the problems of alienated workers to the hazards of unchecked economic growth to a lost respect for nature and the environment to laments over religious or artistic decline. This is not to say that the manifesto touched upon every social problem. In the southern context, racial justice was the most obvious omission. But the scope was so encompassing that the manifesto still defies any conventional classification—whether right or left, radical or reactionary. Take your pick. All fit.

By deciding to drop all specific programs, Ransom left a set of glittering principles that are almost as obvious as respect for motherhood. Of course, all the key words are loaded down with private meanings. One does not have to attach Ransom's ugly images to science or machines or his pleasant ones to nature or to art. But granting his definitions, it is hard to imagine anyone who would dissent from his principles. Their very generality, even vaporous universality, seemed to strip away any very specific content for the word "southern." The lack of specific economic programs made "agrarian" practically a synonym of everything good.

For the reasons cited earlier, the twelve essays did not build consistently upon the opening manifesto. Unlike in Fugitive days, the group was unable to gather and hone all their contributions through debate. Henry B. Kline submitted a rambling monologue not worthy of a "B" in a freshman English class. He decided to write a semiautobiographical account of the experiences of a representative southern exile, one he at first intended to call John Doe. The appalled editors made him change it, and he invented the name William Remington. The summary essay by Stark Young contained a genial series of sermons on the foibles or achievements of southerners, eloquent enough but not consistent with the other essays.

Ransom, Davidson, and Fletcher were most loyal to the manifesto, but even Davidson never fully accepted the hierarchical or feudal social order embraced by Ransom and Fletcher. Thus, attempts to group even three essays soon flounder. Sweeping statements about what all the contributors proposed or wanted are simply not worth the paper they are written on. A brief excursion into the essays at least illustrates this point.[20]

Ransom used his opening, and largely recycled essay, to plug the South into the theoretical framework of the manifesto. He used what Michael O'Brien has correctly described as his "Idea of the South," one only tangentially related to the history of that section and one that Ransom himself referred to as a "southern idea" in contrast to an "American idea." Once again, he pictured the South as an established, ordered, conservative society, one after the European or English model, and one committed to leisure as against profits. This society contrasted with the pioneering, and thus dynamic, mobile, nonestablished, ever-changing, materialistic society of the North, a society given over to economic progress. Ambitious Yankees remained at war with nature, nourished commercial ambitions, and then reaped all the evils of Ransom's industrialism. Now, long after military defeat in the war, the South trembled under a cultural invasion by an alien industrialism. It was at the point of crisis and of choice. Ransom wrote to persuade southerners to fight back, not blindly and belligerently as in the war, but by forming alliances with like-minded people all over the country and then working within the existing political system.[21]

In "Education, Past and Present," Fletcher seemed to share Ransom's vision of an aristocratic and hierarchical society. But in Fletcher the elitism became more belligerent, the tone more reactionary. Fletcher, at least at this point in his confusing intellectual pilgrimage, hated representative democracy and the leveling downward that was, he perceived, an inevitable product of mass public education. He yearned for the old academies, those that educated the rich or the few exceptional and qualified students. He scored some hits, as anyone can, in his identification of the inanities present in any existing school system, but all in all he wanted to return to pauper schools for the masses, those who in a properly ordered society exist only for the sake of their superiors, a statement that soon came back to haunt the other contributors. His bent was to destroy the public schools, but since that was impossible he proposed a second-best solution — the creation of truly elite secondary schools for the few, and the routing of Negroes and less intelligent white children into manual training schools.[22]

Davidson's "A Mirror for Artists" closely paralleled an earlier review in the *Tennessean,* but it well fit *I'll Take My Stand.* In some ways his was the most persuasive essay in the book. He followed up Ransom's argument that industrialism is hostile to the arts, which flourish only in stable, religious, and leisurely societies. In an industrial society the arts may indeed have value — they sell well. But art as a commodity soon ceases to be art as an object of appreciation. In an effective ploy, he joined John Dewey in castigating museums and libraries, those patronized by the wealthy, those which collect and disseminate art and literature as decorative objects to a noncomprehending public. His plea was to make the arts an integral part of life, an adornment of both work and leisure. Mass consumption has severed art from the objects of daily life; specialized factory labor, under the command of bosses, had severed art from work. He believed that over the long term the conditions of modern urban life could not nourish creativity, or when it did survive it would necessarily take a false detour into a type of sick romanticism.

By this approach Davidson was able to say something refreshing about the South, even while admitting its meager past contributions to the more fashionable fine arts. He suggested — with what degree of truth one is hard put to judge — that the Old South, a harmonious agrarian society, and in his view as much or more a democratic than an aristocratic or feudal society (his images came from Middle Tennessee, not from an English gentry), did produce the integrated arts of good living. He stressed, as had Ransom earlier, folk arts, home crafts, oratory, and rustic humor, not "great art," although this might have come later had the war not intervened. Already Davidson rejoiced in the revival of southern literature and in subsequent years celebrated this as if it were a key strategic victory in the ongoing battle of the sections. Self-revealingly, he ended his essay with a note that would have gladdened a Marxist — that the artist, in critical times, cannot separate her art from her larger role as person and citizen. An artist has to fight against the evils that threaten art. She has to join crusades. By implication, even her art is a tool in that larger game, in creating the highest form of beauty, the greatest work of art—a harmonious and fulfilling society. Never again would Davidson separate his politics from his poetry.[23]

Robert Penn Warren would later remember "The Briar Patch" as a defense of segregation. This it was not. In the context of 1930, he took as daring a stand as he could. To put it simply, he argued that the southern Negro would gain more from a continued agricultural economy than from new manufacturing, but only with a major qualification that Warren wanted to emphasize to his white audience. In all areas except social mingling, the Negro had to receive completely equal justice. In effect, Warren threw out the enormous demands implicit in "separate but equal" and, in terms drawn from Booker T. Washington, demanded for blacks the same economic rights, including land ownership, as already enjoyed by whites. Very clear in this essay was an outlook, and a growing sense of guilt, that would soon lead Warren to embrace full racial integration.[24]

Warren's essay, alone, tangled directly with the problem of race. Ransom evaded the issue, but his hierarchical society clearly suggested Negro subordination. In part, his evasion reflected the dominating concerns of time and place. Public awareness of black suppression, at least among whites, reached a record low in the early thirties, as broader economic issues dominated public concern. But in several essays the issue lay just beneath the surface, quite deliberately suppressed or evaded. This most compromised the beguiling moral preferences aired in the book and at least made problematical the various pictures of a South, old or new. From other sources it is clear that in 1930, Owsley, Lytle, and Davidson already took an inflexible stand on segregation and supported this by a belief in some degree of Negro inferiority.[25]

Owsley in his essay developed themes he had explored before Tennessee historians, themes intimately involved in his own scholarship. The times were not propitious for Owsley. He was passed over for department chairman to replace the ailing Vanderbilt dean and historian Walter F. Fleming, to whom *I'll Take My Stand* was dedicated, and had engaged in a vicious fight against Chancellor Kirkland to prevent the appointment of a mediocrity from outside. What came through in Owsley's essay was, on one level, a then conventional historical thesis, one accepted by all the contributors. He argued that the Civil War largely reflected an irrepressible conflict between an industrial North and an agrarian South, or the very theme of much of the symposium. But some of his words were bathed in vitriol, revealing a frustrated, bitterly defensive southerner, an old-fashioned populist who carried a huge personal grudge against the North. The North, in his terms, stood as the perennial imperial aggressor, now bent on the spiritual conquest of the South as well as its continued economic exploitation. He minimized the role of slavery in the road to war, denied it any essential relationship to the southern economy, and referred to "half savage blacks" hardly three generations removed from cannibalism—statements that were not as intentionally mean-spirited as they seemed. Owsley had not yet explored the topic, but he would soon develop his thesis that the backbone of the old South was the small yeoman farmers, those with few or no slaves, and not the few large plantation owners. But in 1930 Owsley was angry and he showed it. Free from the constraints of scholarship, he bared his animus in forceful, pungent prose. As he noted at the Fugitive reunion in 1956, he suffered plenty of scholarly scorn for such bluntness and such honesty.[26]

Poor Allen Tate. He invested so much in the cause. He saw the effort as a defense of religious humanism and chose for himself the critical essay entitled "Remarks on the Southern Religion." But he flubbed the opportunity, ending up with a tense, obscure, often unfocused argument, written in a clever but rather obscure style. His problem was some deep ambivalences about the old South. By 1929, while in France, he was close to converting to Catholicism (he postponed this until 1950). As he reflected on the embryonic "southern movement," he told Ransom that it needed a central or master idea, a type of doctrinal authority, which he wanted to locate in the Christian God and the Roman Catholic Church. He argued that the Church was a source of doctrine "latent" in the southern past, but unfortunately not overt. Most southerners had been Methodists and Baptists, but inappropriately so. The real old southerners had been High Church, really Catholic, all along. For only Catholicism was in accord with the politics and the traditional social order of the old South.[27]

In his labored essay, Tate's first task was to struggle with a definition of religion. Ultimately, he could only clarify an always inadequate verbal definition. Drawing on themes from Ransom, he insisted that true religion, not the attenuated forms that flourished in America, is always holistic, encompassing both the intellectual and experiential aspects of life, the objectified but always inadequate reports about experience and the actual, vital qualities that are experience. He used the awkward image of a horse to make his point—words, abstractions, the sciences deal only with half a horse, with the dynamic and manageable half. A half-horsed religion is one that deals only with how things work. This led him into his understanding of the modern, false religions of production, consumption, and progress.

Next, Tate expanded this whole-part analysis to views of history. The highly abstract long view of the past, which drops out most particularities, is another half horse, as contrasted with the vital, concrete personalities and events present in a short view. The short view alone accommodates the details of religious myth and allows a wholehearted commitment to specific gods or, in brief, to provincial or parochial verities, all of which dissolve in the long view. In all of this Tate revealed his own dilemma, that of one whose intellect led toward the long view, which dissolved traditional loyalties into a type of skepticism or agnosticism, but whose personal needs, and search for identity, pushed him toward the Roman Church. But he wanted to become part of the Church in a natural, simple, mythical, wholehearted way, not in the typical western, defensive way, which leads to elaborate and, to Tate, irrelevant and diverting rationalizations or dogmas. He wanted to be part of a tradition, not argue it or defend it. This put him at cross-purposes with *I'll Take My Stand,* for most of the essays defended both tradition and a particular southern tradition. Painted into a corner, Tate finally and, one feels, with some reluctance, turned to southern religion.[28]

In Tate's view, as necessarily oversimplified, the South developed a feudal economy, one tied to soil and climate, but was never so spiritually isolated as to be able to develop the religion that best fit its social order. In religion it remained part of Protestantism, of a nonagrarian or trading religion, a half-horse religion that served as a mask for secular ambition. The South tried, in vain, to use the catch words of this essentially alien religion to defend their society, but, caught up in contradictions, the South was doomed to defeat. The aggressive North, meantime, developed its own parasitic and imperial society, living economically on such colonies as the South, culturally on England. As Tate put it, New England became a European museum. The South did not borrow from Europe in this way, for in a sense it was Europe, a traditional society rooted in its own native soil. But thus the tragedy—a false religious life, a false mythology, false gods. For rationalization, southerners turned to an artificial rationalism, a rationalism that did not fit their social order any more than the dogmas of fundamentalists provided a fitting religious rationalization. Now, in the crisis of a South under economic and spiritual siege, the section was all but helpless. It had no short view, no mythic resources, no appropriate religion to turn to as a defense. How could the southerner defend himself? Only, said Tate, by violence, by a radical or revolutionary use of political tools to get back to the roots of his heritage. But Tate saw the paradox, if not the helpless obscurity, of this elusive prescription, and ended his essay with the question: could southerners use an alien instrument—politics—to recover a "private, self-contained, and essentially spiritual life?" Clearly Tate doubted it.[29]

The other essays revealed the various linkages and divisions among contributors. Lyle H. Lanier wrote a very balanced, almost scholarly analysis of "The Philosophy of Progress." It included a long, but informed, critique of John Dewey's views and ended with an analysis of the excesses of the new industrial order that would have fit very well into the discussions at a social science convention. In technical terms (clarity, balance) it was the best essay in the volume but did not very clearly advance the philosophical purposes of Ransom. One feels that Lanier, although a native Tennessean and quite loyal to the South, was not so committed to the South as a cause as he was to a more humane economy.[30]

Andrew N. Lytle coined the most memorable title, "The Hind Tit." He used the second half of his long essay to paint a highly idealized verbal portrait of an actual farm in the upper South. In the early, more analytical section he used more pungent language than either Lanier or Ransom to indict the gospel of progress. Like Owsley and Davidson, he pointedly emphasized the yeoman farmers and denied any class rivalry between such farmers and the small numbers of planters. Like Owsley, he also reflected a bit of coun- trified anger at northerners. His essay had one unfortunate effect— it helped people identify the book primarily with subsistence agri- culture and thus helped conceal the more subtle philosophical is- sues that most concerned Ransom and Tate.[31]

Since John Donald Wade was—briefly, as it turned out—in the Vanderbilt English department, he submitted an already completed biographical sketch of "Cousin Lucius." The sketch was based on the life of an uncle, Jacob Walter Frederick, his mother's brother and a former owner of the house Wade and his mother lived in in Marshall- ville, Georgia. By use of the classical and southern name, Lucius, and by emphasis upon a noble and classical hero, Wade turned the largely factual account into the celebration of an ideal but disap- pearing Southern culture, one still worthy of his devotion. In this sense, he exemplified some of the ideals in the opening manifesto.[32]

Herman C. Nixon in "Whither Southern Economy?" resorted to an untypical display of economic statistics. He stuck largely to his- torical description, and presented a series of arguments justifying southern agricultural reform, including the usual plea for greater diversification. He did not oppose manufacturing but only its rapid and unregulated growth, with all the new economic vulnerabilities this entailed. His ideal was a balanced economy, certainly not a fully agricultural one. Little in his essay related him to Ransom, Tate, or Davidson.[33]

Ostensibly, *I'll Take My Stand* was about the South. One could ask: which South? The question might have embarrassed the au- thors. They chose not to address it. Nixon, Owsley, and Davidson, who had read most available literature about the diverse South, ap- preciated the vast economic and cultural differences within even the eleven former Confederate states. And because of two Kentuckians— Tate and Warren—it is not clear that the authors intended such cir- cumscribed borders as the Confederacy. But despite a lack of defini- tion, the essays had plenty of images about a South. A preponder- ance of these clearly fit the upper South, an area dominated by small farms rather than plantations, and a region west of the Ap- palachians, encompassing west and central Kentucky and Tennes- see and northern Georgia, Alabama, and Mississippi. Only Tate was at all conversant with the Chesapeake South, and the Piedmont of the Carolinas, the great manufacturing zone of the South, was almost invisible in the essays. Only rarely did any author refer to the Appalachian South, the South of former unionists and latterday Republicans, let alone to peninsular Florida, French areas of Louisiana, or Hispanic parts of Texas. In fact, almost no references fit the trans-Mississippi South, although Fletcher hailed from Arkansas. Finally, their South was a white South, but a South with a subordinated black minority, not the black-belt South with black majorities. In all these ways the word *South,* when they used it culturally, applied to a very limited South—Anglo-Saxon, formerly Confederate in sympathies, and still agricultural. In fact, even within the geographical borders of the eleven seceding states, it is arguable that the Confederate cause was always a minority cause. Blacks and white unionists, most from the uplands, probably outnumbered the supporters of southern independence.

What seemed most common to the twelve contributors was a view of southern history. The war between the states reflected primarily a competition between two economic systems and ideals— on the one hand an independent yeomanry of farmers and small shopkeepers, on the other a commercial, financial, large manufacturing oligarchy which already dominated the Northeast. The slavery issue provided a convenient, emotionally charged issue, a mere occasion, for a northern, imperial conquest of the South, which almost alone blocked the road to a capitalist future. The war, reconstruction, and subsequent Republican economic policies completed and consolidated the political and economic conquest, leaving the South impoverished, politically impotent, a dependent colony of the North. Such an economic interpretation had plenty of historical support in the thirties. It was reinforced, in the South, by a recognition of southern realities, beginning with incomes at less than half the national average. Equally supportive were the memories, embellished by time, of wartime cruelties or of a purportedly black reconstruction.

The historical myths supported cultural description. All the twelve writers assumed southern distinctiveness, although they would never have agreed on any extended list of defining southern characteristics. But at least four themes pervaded the essays—family, place, leisure, and religion. Southerners, allegedly, have a special relationship to the land, to local space, to roots. They are closely tied to immediate family or to networks of kin. They love leisure. This was the most pregnant term in the book, for it carried such heavy meaning. It identified a nonaggressive, noncommercial culture, one in which people were not grasping, always in a hurry, greedy to make more and more money. Slightly twisted, it involved the old idea of southern laziness. Finally, southerners were more religious than people in other sections of the country, a belief that begged, and rarely received, crucial definitions. In the sophisticated hands of Ransom, this meant that southerners had a fear of, or a sense of dependence upon, nature, and thus reflected a type of awe or piety. For other contributors, the purported religiosity was no more than an empirical judgment, tied to high levels of church membership and the pervasive values of evangelical Protestantism.

I'll Take My Stand was, if nothing else, provocative as well as eloquent. With a few exceptions, such as Kline, the essayists were masters of a sharp, pungent style. To some extent, the beauty of phrase, or a penchant for hyperbole, undermined the serious message they hoped to communicate. One could get lost in the sheer beauty of the language or the vivid images or apt similes. Also, to an immeasurable extent, almost all of the contributors delighted in overstatement, in what they hoped would strike readers as perverse, radical, or shocking. They nourished the image of youthful rebels. Even before critics, to their despair, dismissed them as neo-Confederates, they playfully used such terms for themselves. The playful, satirical, whimsical, or leg-pulling undertone confused readers and invited a lighthearted putdown. Some read the book as half-joke, half *tour de force.*

Few books of the early depression era created quite as much controversy. Every journal or newspaper that could get a copy wrote reviews, until Davidson was able to collect and file over a hundred. The very diversity makes any summary suspect. In a sense, southern reviewers as a whole took the book more seriously and, perhaps because of this, subjected it to the most intense criticism. It ran counter to the industrializing program backed by most large city newspapers in the South. In the North the reviewers more often saw the playful elements in the book or, because of the reputation of the authors, viewed it more as a literary effort. Unfortunately, most newspaper reviewers selected key essays for their analysis and failed to grasp the diversity of content. Except for a few southern reviewers, who caught little but the pro-southern outlook, almost no one endorsed or unqualifiedly praised the book. The one most frequent dissenting view was that industrialism was inevitable, historically necessary even for the South, and that only fools essayed to stop it. The only negotiable policy issue was how to discipline or control or ameliorate it. Thus, the Agrarians were utopians, nostalgic eccentrics, or literary dreamers, lost in wistful thinking. Despite the deliberate perversity of their effort, the Agrarians had hoped for more praise. Sensitive ones, like Davidson, felt hurt at the response and became bitter when, as one might have expected, the reviewers never seemed to get the point. But what point? Here is where the hidden fissures misled each author. Each had a slightly different agenda, and thus no reviewer could possibly please all contributors. The content was not only too rich but contained too many unblendable ingredients.[34]

For this reason, the book has endured. It continuously takes on new meaning and appeals to new audiences. Like a well-cut diamond, the various facets of the book alternately flash with every shift in the position of the cultural sun. In the 1950s, intellectuals lamented the advent of a mass society, of plastic other-directed people, of conformity and mediocrity, of lagging educational standards, of a society given over to quantity at the expense of quality. Just what the Agrarians had prophesied. In the sixties rural poverty became a national embarrassment. Political rebels now charted the evils of monopoly capitalism, consoled alienated workers or students who had to cope with large, impersonal managers, and tried to escape from false, consumer values. I'll Take My Stand became a campus bestseller, appealing both to campus radicals and to advocates of a counterculture. In the early seventies concern shifted to people's alienation from nature, to their distorting role in the environment, and to the need for ecological balance and a regained respect for the earth. And no one had expressed these sentiments more eloquently than the Vanderbilt Agrarians. Finally, by the late seventies and early eighties, Americans tried to adjust to energy shortages, to the prospect of depleted resources, and suddenly realized the waste involved in large cities and their mad rush to ever higher levels of consumption. Conservation became a watchword. A new generation at least yearned for a return to the land; homesteading once again became fashionable. Folk arts revived, and sheepish suburbanites began growing gardens and burning wood. Small is beautiful! And all right out of *I'll Take My Stand,* by then clearly one of the most influential documents of cultural dissent in American history.[35]

IV.

The Movement

For the three most involved contributors—Ransom, Davidson, and Tate—*I'll Take My Stand* was to be only the opening salvo in a much larger crusade. Periodicals, newspapers, political action, and a possible academy had been their long-term goals. Briefly, for at least a few heady months after the appearance of the book, the larger dream still seemed compelling, at least in part realizable. But in less than a year the thrill, the excitement faded. Resignation, even despair set in, although the Nashville Agrarians continued to meet, to party, and to talk. Yet, so often, they could only commiserate with each other at the lack of any major, practical progress. The developing great depression seemed to vindicate the prophetic message of *I'll Take My Stand,* but it also began to exact its high personal costs. By the fall of 1931, most of the Agrarians had to give almost all their attention to earning a living or to keeping their families together. Yet, some of the agrarian ardor lived on. The group kept looking for a new outlet, a new program. This arrived in 1933 in a new publishing venture, paralleling what seemed, briefly at least, a promising shift in American politics because of the new Democratic administration. The brethren rallied, took heart, and launched a new crusade, one more practical and more overtly political than the one in 1929–30. Out of this would develop a true agrarian program, one tied to land reform and property restoration. By the most precise use of the terms, a southern agrarian movement was born only in 1933 and burned itself out over the next four years. Unlike the book, this movement has received scant attention from historians and literary critics.

In the immediate aftermath of the publication of *I'll Take My Stand,* the Nashville Agrarians plunged into a frenzy of activities. In November 1930, at Richmond, Virginia, Ransom debated String-fellow Barr, editor of the *Virginia Quarterly Review.* He had been rejected as a contributor to *I'll Take My Stand* when he would not accept the manifesto. Sherwood Anderson, moderating before an audience of 3,000, clearly took Ransom's side. Ransom read a de-fense of the book. In a more informal way, Barr took pot-shots at the book, or ridiculed what he saw as its more wild and fanciful claims. Allen and Caroline Tate attended, voting Ransom a clear winner. Subsequently, in New Orleans and at Sewanee, Ransom debated William Knickerbocker, editor of the *Sewanee Review* and one of the most eloquent and persuasive critics of *I'll Take My Stand,* which he took seriously and understood quite well. Ransom also debated the cynical editor of a Macon, Georgia, newspaper at a four-day conference at Emory University. Warren refused oppor-tunities to debate the book but, from his temporary teaching posi-tion in Memphis, tried to arrange a debate for Ransom. Davidson took the debate platform against Knickerbocker only once, down in Columbia, Tennessee, before almost all the agrarian brethren, who drove down as if to a football game. Of course, from their perspective, they always bested their critics.[1]

In November and December 1930, as the largely harsh or satiri-cal reviews poured in, Tate fell into near despair. He reacted in an-ger ("this is war") and in a periodical bout of radical denunciations. He wanted to fight back, to get the agrarian journal launched. He rallied Davidson, Ransom, Lytle, and Lanier at a meeting to form a new agrarian party on November 22. Which five gathered is sig-nificant. Although Wade did not attend, he was at Vanderbilt and included in the committees established at this organizational meet-ing. Yet one feels he was never so deeply, emotionally committed as the other five. Warren was then in Memphis, at Southwestern, but would return to Vanderbilt in the fall of 1931 as an instructor in the Vanderbilt English department. This move, and his personal affection for Tate and Ransom, pulled him back into the agrarian circle. Owsley had suffered a near–nervous breakdown that fall, and for a time could not join the crusade. As he later put it, "I blew all my fuses and shot my bearings," but within a year he was back in the harness, one of the leaders in this true agrarian effort. Fletcher and Nixon were in Arkansas and Louisiana, respectively, but at the time both would probably have joined had they been able to participate. Even counting them, the twelve had already shrunk to ten. Young contributed to *I'll Take My Stand* but never endorsed the agrarian cause. After his weak essay, the group largely ignored Kline, who was in Knoxville and never in any sense a part of what they soon called the brotherhood. Thus, for the next few years, ten people, and only eight in Nashville, would keep the faith, support the elusive cause.[2]

The new agrarian party never survived its first meeting. Committees to investigate the purchase of a county newspaper (Lytle and Tate), to organize the second symposium (Tate, Davidson, and Ransom), to issue press releases, to arrange debates, or rebut attacks (Ransom and Lanier), and to organize public meetings and rally supporters (Davidson, Lytle, and Wade) never functioned as far as any records indicate. By December, Tate, backed by Ransom, had prepared a tentative grant proposal to the Guggenheim Foundation to fund some of the planned new ventures. But Davidson, leery of northern money, refused to sign the application and the others reluctantly dropped the idea. This was a straw in the wind, a sign of deep fissures among the brethren, but mutual forbearance postponed any serious internal conflict.[3]

By the spring of 1931, the zest and enthusiasm began to wane. For two frustrating years, none of the brethren were able to do much to advance the cause. Even the level of writing, of reviews and articles, declined to a record low for such normally productive authors. The depression played a major role, creating financial hardship for both Tate and Davidson. Publishers were wary of book contracts, even as outlets for articles shrank yearly. And in the depression no one had any money to launch new journals or newspapers. For years, Tate talked to his businessman brother Ben about a literary journal, but they never moved beyond preliminary planning. Sheer necessity forced each of the Agrarians to attend to his own career, almost to the exclusion of agrarian agitation, which by 1932 seemed to have been a wonderful luxury, a youthful indulgence in the more prosperous times. To keep up the fight in the worst of times simply required more personal sacrifices, more threats to growing families, than anyone dared risk. As Davidson soon lamented—when the chips were down, they were not as committed rebels as they had wanted to be. They had played at revolution on weekends or confused real activism with mere academic gains.[4]

The Nashville group remained together. If anything, adversity strengthened the personal bonds among the eight. In later years, most looked back on the early thirties, in spite of the depression, as a golden interlude, one blessed by wonderful comradeship, fascinating parties, and a fulfilling sense of community. The chief arbiter of the fellowship was Allen Tate. In the summer of 1930 the Tates moved into a historic, refurbished farmhouse on the south bank of the Cumberland River, just across and upriver from Clarksville, Tennessee, and only forty miles from Nashville. Since Tate's brother Ben bought the farm, Caroline soon dubbed it Benfolly, a name that gained national fame among writers in the depression. This noncommercial farm was within fifteen miles of Robert Penn Warren's family home in Guthrie and close to Caroline's Meriwether clan. The Tates would live here for the next two years and then intermittently through 1937. They never really farmed but kept a cow, gardened a bit, and tried (almost disastrously) to supervise a young couple in a tenant cottage.

If their apartments in New York had been a way station for young writers, then Benfolly was a resort. It became a depression mecca, a place of hospitality, fellowship, and brilliant conversation for dozens of writers, some famous, some obscure. Each spring and again in the early fall it operated almost like a hotel, with all the rooms and beds filled with guests. Some, like Ford Madox Ford, brought a wife and stayed the whole summer. Warren and his wife, Cinina, came whenever possible. Others, such as Hart Crane, Edmund Wilson, Louise Bogan, Katherine Anne Porter, Stark Young, Howard Baker, Phelps Putnam (all guests in 1931), plus spouses or mistresses, a wandering philosopher from Ohio State, even a sculptor sent by Ransom to do Tate's profile, came and stayed for days or even weeks. In the final summer of 1937, when the Fords were in residence and the house already full, a youthful, rebellious Robert Lowell came, as he said, to learn to write. The Tates not only tolerated youthful indiscretions (on arrival he urinated on the front gate), but allowed him to live in a tent in the yard, taking meals with the whole assembly. Caroline tried to cope, at least when the Tates could afford servants, which by early 1932 was never. During the worst, she could escape to her nearby Meriwether relatives, where she could at times borrow Negro servants or beg needed food.[5]

In the dark years of 1931 and 1932 the agrarian brethren gathered whenever possible at Benfolly, particularly during the winter months, when they were teaching and the European and New York crowd stayed away. The two "boys," Lytle and Warren, were practically family members. On weekends Davidson (rarely Teresa), the Ransoms, the Laniers, and the Owsleys would also join in parties, picnics, late-night drinking bouts, endless games of charades, interlaced with deep and solemn agrarian conspiracies. Wade was less a part of the social group. Davidson, who later wrote a poem to celebrate these wonderful Benfolly gatherings in the large ground-floor dining room with its great fireplace (the mantel had a .22 rifle and a Confederate flag), was actually the most reticent—less one of the boys, less rowdy and Bohemian, than even the proper Ransom. On occasion, the Tates drove down to Nashville for a round of parties at various homes or to play poker with a club that met at the Laniers'.[6]

The eight writers retained their special leadership role, but the agrarian circle was much larger. Several Nashville friends or converts joined in the parties, creating an enlarged circle of at least twenty. Two Vanderbilt librarians were especially supportive—Isabelle Howell and Frances Cheney. Howell was for years a close friend of the Owsleys and a frequent companion of the unmarried Lytle. Cheney, along with her husband, Brainerd (Lon) Cheney, a distinguished writer himself, converted fully to a version of Agrarianism and, as of 1987, continue to defend it. Eventually, several members of the Vanderbilt English department converted, at least in part, to agrarian beliefs, with Richard C. Beatty, a biographer, often listed by the Agrarians as a close ally. In a sense, Cleanth Brooks, a former Vanderbilt student, a Rhodes scholar, a poet and critic, and eventually a colleague and coeditor with Warren at Louisiana State

University, became an adopted or latter-day Agrarian. The spouses also played a vital role. Caroline Gordon could claim as much success as a writer as any of the men. In a sense she was the Louisa May Alcott of Agrarianism, with her wry, realistic commentary on the romantic flights and near inanities of the brethren. The group considered her as a possible contributor to *I'll Take My Stand* (she was too skeptical to be an Agrarian) and expressed pride in her achievements as a novelist. They always listed her among leading southern writers but did not try to enlist her for their political battles. In this area, Agrarianism remained an all-masculine movement.

The fun and games at Benfolly helped mask a period of frustration and nonwriting for Tate. He had a contract for a biography of Robert E. Lee but slowly bogged down in the research. He could not find a way through the complexities and pitfalls of Lee's life and by 1931 was just spinning his wheels, even as Caroline finally finished her first novel, *Penhally,* one based on local characters and with a Civil War setting. By the end of 1931, Tate was broke, almost desperate. Increasingly, he was disillusioned with Davidson, in some ways his closest friend. A cosmopolitan Tate feared that Davidson, in his melancholy and near paranoia, was retreating into a narrow, dogmatic provincialism. For example, in December 1931, Tate wanted the Agrarians as a group to join in a petition, circulated by Theodore Dreiser, in support of writers indicted under a criminal syndicalism law in Tate's home state of Kentucky. Admittedly, the Communist Party made this a *cause célèbre,* but Tate wanted to enlist Agrarians in the cause of free speech. Davidson refused. He did not want to support either Dreiser or writers who had allegedly incited miners in eastern Kentucky. Tate saw this as a symptom of an overly defensive, dying Agrarianism. He tried to write poems and temporarily gave up on the agrarian movement. Then, most depressing of all, in May 1932, his old friend Hart Crane committed suicide by jumping from a ship in the Caribbean.[7]

In 1932 Caroline, on the basis of her much acclaimed first novel, won a Guggenheim fellowship. The $2,000 rescued the Tates from imminent bankruptcy, although it proved barely sufficient for another penurious year in Europe. In April they rented Benfolly and sailed on a cheap mail boat ($180 round-trip) for England and France. The Laniers traveled with them, and the Owsleys were also in France during the same period. Ransom was just returning from a sabbatical in England, so desperate for money that he had to beg a special loan from Chancellor Kirkland to get his family back to Nashville. For a time, Agrarianism seemed to move across the Atlantic. For Ransom, Tate, and Owsley, European contacts proved critical in stimulating new intellectual interests, or what amounted to new meanings for their Agrarianism.

In a resumed correspondence, Tate and Davidson soon began a morbid analysis of agrarian backsliding and tried to gather courage for an agrarian revival. Davidson, as always complaining of overwork and illness, lamented what he saw as the waning loyalty of the brethren. He admitted that they had not risked all; that, being married, with wives and children, they had been reluctant to take risks, to lose the security of jobs, to battle to the death. They had not really charged the breastworks of industrialism, and even their writing, their only weapons so far, had slowed to a trickle. He urged a new, programmatic symposium, a larger agrarian meeting, a weekly journal, and some form of agrarian organization with more and better essays in its defense.[8]

Tate was stung by the implied charge of near apostasy. In response he lamented the diversions of Ransom into peripheral economic issues and gave his diagnosis of why *I'll Take My Stand* had such limited impact. It had been too English and too full of Anglonostalgia (Ransom and Fletcher), too oriented to tradition and not enough related to contemporary southern problems (ironic, for Tate had helped push the European themes). But beyond that, the Agrarians had not believed deeply enough in the cause. It was not a religion for them, and only a religion could inspire the needed enthusiasm. The movement had degenerated into pleasant poker games on Saturday night. He was also bitter because he had moved back to the South in behalf of the cause and been let down. But he believed that events had vindicated their stand and the time was right for new, effective blows.[9] Broke, but finally free of the Lee biography (he decided to repudiate the contract), back to writing again, Tate returned to America in March 1933, in time to learn of a new publishing offer from an old, at times resented New York publisher, Seward Collins, editor of the literary journal, the *Bookman*. This offer in a short time reinvigorated the Agrarian movement, with Tate the point man, the contact with the larger cosmopolitan world, but once again not the most important idea man.

If possible, Davidson suffered through two more difficult years than Tate. He kept his job at Vanderbilt and with it a modicum of family security. But he hated the drudgery of freshman English. In late 1930 the *Tennessean* dropped its book page, a casualty of the bankruptcy of the huge investment firm, Caldwell & Company, and the disgrace and ultimate imprisonment of publisher Luke Lea. This almost halved Davidson's income and forced him to seek other jobs. He would find a substitute, one pregnant with implications for his subsequent career, when he won a summer position in 1931, at the Bread Loaf Writers' Conference in Vermont, which soon became one of the most prestigious schools for writers in the country. Sponsored by Middlebury College, graced annually by the poet Robert Frost, it became a separate, alternative career for Davidson, entailing a radical shift in environment and role each year. Amazingly, for such a fervent southerner, he loved Vermont, and soon began writing long, perceptive sketches of this lovely souvenir of an older, orderly, Puritan culture, so much the opposite of what he knew in the South. At times he loved Vermont so much that he became overly critical of the South and at least personally must have flirted with thoughts of emigration. He taught summers in Vermont until 1967, eventually bought a home near Bread Loaf, and after retirement from Vanderbilt spent up to half of each year in New England. Vermont forced on Davidson a realization, already implicit in his writings about southern literature, that the United States was not really a nation, but a congeries of very distinct regions, each with a holistic and, short of outside intervention, a healthy culture. Such regions were threatened by an imposed, uniform national culture. Large, centralized firms had tried to push such a culture upon the vulnerable, exploited, outlying regions, such as New England or the South. A second threat to such regions was the uniform policy of a strong, central government, the modern and ever-threatening leviathan.

Back at Vanderbilt in the fall of 1931, Davidson suffered the worst year of his life, one that left him ill and close to a mental breakdown. He and his wife had lived in an apartment in Wesley Hall, home of Vanderbilt's Divinity School. It burned in February 1932, destroying their furniture and most of Davidson's books. Briefly, they and their daughter were charity cases. He felt lonely, deserted, a frequent malady for Davidson. And nothing was happening on the agrarian front. He turned back to poetry and fretted until his summer job in Vermont. By then Tate was in France, Ransom just back from England. Davidson could not face another academic year at Vanderbilt and could not get a paid leave from the university. For unclear reasons, he was reluctant to apply for outside grants. Thus, he accepted an invitation from his friend John Wade to spend an academic year in a small but adequate guest house behind the Wade family home in Marshallville, Georgia. Wade, meantime, was back at Vanderbilt teaching.

Marshallville, in a peach-growing, fertile area of central Georgia, confronted Davidson with what he soon took to be the real South, the South of former cotton plantations, of a settled owning class, and a majority population of working blacks. The local townspeople, because of respect for its leading family, the Wades, because of Davidson's poetic accomplishments, and because of his sweet and gentle demeanor, treated him like a king. He relaxed, felt loved and appreciated, gave plenty of speeches, made lasting friends, and soon dubbed this fertile and friendly land a modern Eden. Almost every year for the rest of Wade's life, Davidson would visit Marshallville, at least briefly. The year restored his confidence, encouraged a new burst of writing, and whetted a long-term interest in folk music. He visited, and exalted in, old harp singing at a rural church, and would soon love nothing as much as the ballads and church music preserved from British sources in the backwoods of the South. He soon became one of America's most perceptive folklorists.

Davidson found in and around Marshallville an intact, rooted regional culture as vital and appealing as the very different one he knew in Vermont. To him, this culture seemed ideal typical southern, much more so than the more Yankee-influenced upper South of Middle Tennessee. Within two years he would compose his most popular, much revised, and endlessly anthologized essay, one of the greatest literary products of the agrarian impulse, "Still Rebels, Still Yankees." In the final half of it he drew a loving, carefully nuanced portrait of the typical Yankee, Brother Jonathan (based on Homer

Noble, the Vermont farmer with whom the Davidsons boarded in early Vermont trips and upon whose land Frost built his famous cabin), and the typical southerner, Cousin Roderick (based on a neighbor and friend of John Wade's).[10]

By 1933, Davidson had his fixed orientation toward the South and his own distinct version of Agrarianism. It overlapped the views of other brethren in some of its implied programs and thus allowed Davidson to remain a vital, at times the most fervent, member of the agrarian circle. For him Agrarianism became a synonym for his brand of regionalism. Since so many writers of the thirties discovered regional differences, or tried to shape federal policies to fit regional needs, Davidson seemed to be on the cutting edge of social thought. But he scarcely appreciated the new respect, although he exploited it to place articles and to win a contract for a book of essays, *The Attack on Leviathan* (1938). He carried on a continuing and at times friendly dialogue with Howard Odum and other North Carolina social scientists who popularized a form of regionalism. Davidson appreciated their detailed scholarship, found useful their definitions of regional boundaries, drew endlessly upon their statistical surveys, supported their efforts to find local answers to pressing economic problems, and shared their desire to find decentralized modes for administering federal policies.[11]

But Odum and his colleagues wanted to disinfect regionalism of sectional partisanship or, in Davidson's eyes, to defuse it of its radical political implications. Sectionalism was only the political side of regionalism. For the next decade Davidson would replace the popular Marxist class analysis, and class politics, with an equally radical sectional politics. To him, economic exploitation was the critical problem of modern America, but this exploitation was reflected not in the predations of an owning class but in the imperial machinations of a dominant section—the industrialized North, centered in the financial and commercial capital of New York City, and increasingly abetted by a growing federal government which, behind the welfare nostrums of the New Deal, he viewed as a captive, an agent, of this sectionally-based industrial capitalism. Thus, capitalists and Washington bureaucrats were linked evils and, for the South, the only defense had to be an aggressive, politically-charged resistance movement, even to the point of guerrilla warfare if that were necessary. For the preindustrial South, the Marxist class analysis did not fit; class feelings had not yet developed and would develop only in the wake of industrialism. Odum and other mild regionalists, who tried to work with the New Deal, to find unifying national motifs to avoid sectional conflict, had, in their placid and compromising liberalism, forgotten the results of the Civil War and ignored the desperate colonial status of the modern South. Davidson, in this sense, wanted to reopen the struggle of 1861 and to gain a type of economic and cultural independence for the South, or the political side of any honest and courageous regionalism. [12]

None of the other Agrarians fully agreed with Davidson. Owsley came closest, but with a difference. Owsley bet his heart and soul on the Roosevelt administration, whereas Davidson was leery of the New Deal by 1934, completely disillusioned by 1936 (he cast a reluctant vote for Roosevelt, his last support for a national Democrat), and a bitter enemy of Roosevelt's version of the leviathan from then on. Owsley agreed with, or in effect supplied Davidson with, most of his historical ammunition about the colonial South, a theme also well developed by Charles A. Beard and even full-fledged Marxist historians. But Owsley hoped to gain southern goals through a friendly, Democratic administration, and enthusiastically supported New Deal economic programs, beginning with agricultural credit and price subsidies. Even so, with Davidson, he soon glimpsed another side to the New Deal, a side represented by social scientific planners, by labor union leaders, and by Eleanor Roosevelt and other do-gooders. This politics of central economic planning, or of social reform, threatened southern interests, most of all its racial policies. Owsley worked to keep the New Deal on track—restraint on threatening social legislation but radical or populistic economic measures to help the impoverished and depressed South. Owsley wanted government ownership of utilities and possibly those industries that were naturally, or already, dominated by large firms. He also soon embraced extreme land reform proposals for the South, an aggressive and radical form of true agrarianism.

Herman Clarence Nixon joined Owsley in the early thirties on economic policies. He was an equally enthusiastic supporter of Roosevelt and the New Deal. So long as the two old Alabama friends corresponded about economic policies, they seemed as one, and they viewed Davidson as at least a close ally, one willing to consider radical economic alternatives even if suspicious of too much government intervention. From a distance, John Gould Fletcher, himself pulled in varied economic directions, referred, with some justification, to Owsley, Nixon, Davidson, and himself as left-wing agrarians, over against the largely cultural concerns he attributed, not quite correctly, to Tate, Ransom, Lytle, Wade, and Warren. But again the alliance was fragile. Nixon, as his friends failed to grasp until after 1935, supported Roosevelt's social legislation as fervently as his economic. Also, unlike Davidson and Owsley, he applied both a sectional and a class analysis to southern problems and was soon as aware of exploitation of southerners by southerners as by northern imperialists. He tried to fan class feeling in the South and wanted a class politics, a rallying of poor whites and blacks against local and distant oppressors, a political strategy that soon led him into a working partnership with American socialists and even Communist party members.

Above all, what separated Nixon from Davidson and Owsley were his views on race. Nixon wanted to form an alliance of blacks and whites, and as a goal, even as an eventual necessity for a just South, wanted to get rid of the caste system, to gain racial equality, though these issues were not so much in the foreground of his concerns in the early thirties. Owsley and Davidson, with at least equal intensity, felt threatened by any federal policies that touched upon the existing racial settlement in the South. Both, for reasons deep and often ill-rationalized, identified southern civilization with white dominance and Negro subordination. In the crunch they would sacrifice every other economic and social goal, even to the extent of shifting over to their industrial enemies, if this proved necessary to preserve white supremacy. In the showdown race was the defining essence of their South. And, eventually, Lytle would agree with them.

From 1931 to 1933, Ransom traveled a very different path from Davidson and Owsley. He would soon draw Tate into his economic prescriptions, but Tate never made economic programs so central as did Ransom, who was almost obsessed with them for an interlude of three or four years. The depression, the plight of southerners by 1931, the suffering of small farmers, and the millions of unemployed all dismayed Ransom. He wanted solutions. In one of the periodic and major shifts of interest and scholarly engagement that typified his career, he became a lay economist, giving himself as fully to his new mistress as he had given himself to poetry in the early twenties and to the cultural requirements of religion and art in the late twenties.

In 1931, Ransom began long conversations with Vanderbilt economists. He read, with approval, a few back-to-the-land schemes pushed in America during the early depression, including one by the popular journalist Bernarr MacFadden in his *Liberty* magazine that led to important bills before Congress. Then, in the fall of 1931, he moved to England on a Guggenheim grant, and spent much of his time there working on an economic treatise, first entitled "Capitalism and Land" and later just "Land," which he submitted without success to publishers. In odd moments he advocated other economic nostrums, such as a relocated national capitol (to create new jobs), or a vast international scholarly exchange program as a way of solving the international debt problem (a close parallel to the later Fulbright program). In Britain, Ransom met with intellectuals who shared his concerns, joined in a lecture tour with Christopher Dawson, a friend of T. S. Eliot's, and read the works of Hilaire Belloc and G. K. Chesterton, who, along with their disciples, supported the small reform movement called Distributism. He also submitted portions of his new economic treatise to British economists, usually eliciting a less-than-enthusiastic response. He made endless revisions, some required by the rapidly shifting economic and political situation in Europe and America. He would eventually give up in frustration and destroy the manuscript. But at least two articles, as well as his letters to Tate, clarify what he was about.[13]

Ransom soon came to believe that America's ample supply of land offered a solution to the ills of depression and unemployment. His analysis, influenced by the critical advice of economists, became quite sophisticated and subtle. He offered a strictly economic solution, one tied to the primary needs of people to have a job and enough to eat. His solution involved a partial return to subsistence farming, both by beleaguered commercial farmers and by the unemployed in cities, but he tried to mute what he called the virtues of farm life, the esthetic and spiritual benefits. He wanted a hardheaded answer. At the same time, he departed from, and would never return to, several themes in *I'll Take My Stand*. He now embraced a much more equalitarian approach, one that he often attributed to Jefferson and to the guiding ideals of the early American republic. No longer did he talk of a European model or of an aristocratic and hierarchical society. In ignoring, if not repudiating, these critical themes, he moved closer to the equalitarian, yeoman perspective of Owsley, Lytle, and Davidson. By the early thirties the elitist and aristocratic motifs in *I'll Take My Stand* had become such an embarrassment that Davidson tried to excuse, or dismiss as personal idiosyncrasies, the more arrogant passages of Fletcher's education essay.

Ransom's proposed solution soon had many advocates, but he felt that sentimental back-to-the-landers, like Ralph Borsodi, did not have the required economic analyses to support their schemes. One practical outgrowth of such thinking, which appealed to Franklin D. Roosevelt, would be a small Division of Subsistence Homesteads in the early New Deal. All the Agrarians rejoiced at the early, decentralized program, which led to over thirty small communities, made up in most cases of small subsistence plots tied to planned small industries, many of which never materialized. Even before this program was absorbed in 1935 by the Resettlement Administration, which largely replaced the subsistence motif in its new communities by cooperative farming, it had, almost as a necessity, moved to more centralized control from Washington, a centralization that disillusioned Davidson and several of the brethren. By 1935 only Nixon remained a fervent supporter of such resettlement schemes. Even before the organizational changes of 1935, Ransom tried to disassociate himself from one goal embedded in this early government-sponsored back-to-the-land scheme—to merge part-time, subsistence farming with part-time employment in manufacturing, a farm and factory scheme advocated by Henry Ford as well as by several New Deal officials.

Ransom tried to chart, in detail, recent shifts in the American economy. In both agriculture and manufacturing, the United States had moved toward a highly specialized, highly centralized, market and money-oriented, interdependent system, or what he now referred to not as industrialism but as capitalism. Since American farmers had never been subsistence farmers and had always produced products for sale, they had fully participated in these changes, moving toward an efficient, capital-intensive production of single crops. This was a more efficient agriculture, linked with a steadily growing surplus of people not needed on the farm who flocked in World War I and the twenties into the cities, there finding jobs more rewarding than their low-paid agricultural labors. Thus, the number of farmers steadily declined, even as agricultural production increased, leading to surpluses, low prices, and, ironically, even a surplus of land, for the new farming concentrated on the best soils, leaving a large margin of good but unneeded farm land for recreational uses or no use at all. But demand had lagged, and the supplies of all products had saturated markets.

Ransom, confused by the various analyses of different economists, never tried to explain the great depression. He took it as a fact, believed, as did so many in the thirties, that it would be years before demand would catch up with supplies (he did agree that this would probably happen in the future), and that suffering Americans required an early solution. His answer was obvious from the analysis—to move people back onto the waiting land and drastically to increase the subsistence aspects of American agriculture. Existing farmers, burned by market dependency and the collapse of credit, should direct labor not only into subsistence foods but into an array of services they had bought from the outside. Unemployed workers, particularly those with farming skills, should move back to the land and take up the same type of farming. Unfortunately, the service side of agriculture had also changed, away from the small shops and stores of local towns to branches of large, national chains, leading to the decline, or helpless dependence, of so many people in small rural towns. As much as possible, Ransom wanted to decentralize the service of agriculture and move back, not only toward more subsistence farming, but to stronger, less dependent, more regional marketing systems, to the type of rural economy that prevailed in the late nineteenth century.

Ransom's endless qualifications rescued his argument from romantic fancy. He stressed that the new or, as he called them, agrarian farmers would not try to supply all their own needs. They would continue to sell produce on the market, perhaps almost as much as before, but they would be less dependent on such sales. Also, he stressed that he did not want farmers to go back to primitive methods. Just the opposite. To the extent that they could afford it, short of mortgages, and as soon as they could afford it, he wanted them to utilize all the scientific benefits available, from electricity to the latest techniques to the best seeds and fertilizers to the most modern machinery. He did not advocate a less scientific agriculture or any loss of the conveniences of modern farming. At the same time, he realized that most of the industrial, market-oriented, urban economy would have to continue. Thus, he sheepishly admitted to Tate that, to an extent, he had already deserted the agrarian cause, for he was no longer opposed to all industrialism. Even his agrarian farmers still needed someone to buy their products and to provide them with manufactured goods. Most city workers would continue to work for wages and to buy their food. A market for farm produce was assured, but a somewhat smaller market than needed to absorb existing production. Thus, the move back to subsistence would divert labor away from market crops and, he hoped, reduce production to the level of demand. Finally, such a partially subsistence but still commercial agriculture would be able to absorb many of the unemployed, and in such a way as not to threaten the jobs of anyone else.

Ransom's older ideals did inform a bit of his analysis. For example, he advised against part-time industrial employment for such farmers. It would be distracting, create ambivalence, and lessen their independence. As he saw it, farmers could find plenty of work even in the winter months, as they attended to repairs, carried out small manufacturing, and lessened their dependence on outside artisans or retail shops. And Ransom, in a typical stance, hypothesized that this agriculture might salvage for them, in off seasons, a desired leisure, for hunting, fishing, or typical agrarian forms of meditation. In this way, the land could support a noble American ideal—the sustenance of homes and homemaking, of independent proprietors, or ideals underlaying the development of the early American Republic.[14]

The other brethren were not idle, but neither Lytle, Lanier, Wade, nor Warren developed new agrarian theories or tactics. Lytle, whose views seemed closest to Davidson's, was socially closer to Tate and Warren. Though no longer the kid, he still delighted the older brethren by his several courtships, received their sympathies for the death of his mother and threats to the Alabama farm owned by his father, and launched his literary career with publication of a spirited biography of Nathan Bedford Forrest in 1931. By 1933 he was at work on his first novel, *The Long Night,* which not only would be based on true stories about relatives of Frank Owsley but was for a while a cooperative venture. Lanier, along with Ransom, became deeply involved in Vanderbilt academic politics but did not publish any new agrarian essays. A talented Wade gently supported the other Agrarians, at times marveled at but could not share their energy or their political zeal, and was content to offer small suggestions or to continue his subtle jabs at the arrogance and pretension of a predominant urban culture.

Warren from 1931 to 1934 struggled to live on a meager instructor's salary at Vanderbilt, all the while seeking a secure academic job elsewhere. In the midst of poverty, and despite the trials of his often ailing wife, he still managed to finish an early draft of his first novel, *Night Riders,* in 1933. For 1933–34, after desperate efforts to find a new job, and almost begging pleas to Mims, he gained a part-time position in the Vanderbilt English department, one increased to full time in the spring because Wade resigned his position at Vanderbilt to return to the University of Georgia. By then, Tate and Owsley were quite sure that Mims and old Chancellor Kirkland had joined in a conspiracy, not only to be rid of Warren but slowly to starve him to death. During these difficult years, Warren found needed emotional sustenance among the brethren, loved them all for their friendship, and wrote some delightfully sympathetic but whimsical essays about the Agrarians. Never in all the agrarian years, though, did he ever write a single essay in which he committed himself, philosophically, to any version of agrarian ideology. Rather, he wrote on literature, including some defenses of southern writers, and on the artistic potential of a still largely agricultural South.

By the spring of 1933, the basis of a new agrarian crusade was in place. For quite divergent reasons, at least five of the continuing Agrarians had developed clear political commitments—Tate, Owsley, Nixon, Davidson, and Ransom. Their differences still left a point of convergence. By 1933 they began to recognize this and to defer in appropriate ways to the distinctive emphases and concerns of each other. In particular, they all deferred to Davidson's region-alism; Ransom even wrote an essay on the esthetics of regionalism. The main point of convergence was the old proprietary ideal, so cen-tral, if often only implicit, in most of the essays in *I'll Take My Stand*. At the heart of all their goals was property, or at least a type of property—land or other means of production under the full man-agerial control of the individual owners. Such proprietorship was indispensable to the programs designed by each of these five men, not less so for the populist restoration of Nixon and Owsley, or the regional autonomy of Davidson, than for the subsistence agriculture of Ransom. Thus, by 1933 the Agrarians had discovered property—a momentous discovery, as it turned out—and the restoration of property became their only unifying goal for a new, quite practical and quite political agrarian crusade. But this crusade awaited both a new publishing outlet and the support of other like-minded re-formers. The catalyst for both of these was an eccentric, ideologi-cally volatile, and untrustworthy Seward Collins.

In a sense, history repeated itself. In 1930, Tate returned home from his Guggenheim in France and quickly secured a contract for *I'll Take My Stand*. In March 1933 he once again sailed back to New York City and almost immediately helped consummate a new pub-lishing scheme with Collins and the *Bookman*. Collins made the original overtures. He wanted to revive his lagging journal and, in fact, would soon decide to start it anew as the *American Review*. Collins, as Tate knew from several earlier and at times unpleasant encounters, could be eccentric and unreliable. He was given to in-tellectual enthusiasms, pursued with more zeal than wisdom. But he had a journal, and the Agrarians had floundered for three years without any reliable publishing outlet. What Collins had noted in the early depression was the increased relevance and appeal of vari-ous antimodernist movements. An earlier fan of Babbitt and More, he now wanted to form an alliance of New Humanists, Agrarians, English Distributists, and other small groups, some tied to the Cath-olic Church, some, like Ralph Borsodi, supporting practical back-to-the-land schemes. Such an editorial stance could give cohesion to a new review journal and seemed certain to appeal to some of the most eminent and eloquent Anglo-American writers, possibly including T. S. Eliot (he wrote for it). But, perhaps to Collins's later regret, he first approached the better organized Agrarians, talking directly to Tate in New York. All this led to a plan for a meeting with all the brethren. Before it was over, the Agrarians made a bid to capture Collins and, in effect, turn the *American Review* into their own periodical.

The big meeting with Collins, after one postponement, took place on 6–7 April 1933, at Cornsilk, the Lytle farm in Alabama. All eight brethren attended. Davidson came up from Marshallville. Nixon, although not invited, was still valued as a likely contributor to a new symposium and soon, by letter, waxed enthusiastic about the new agrarian crusade. The unfortunate Fletcher who, had he the chance, would have been there come hell or high water, was in a hospital in Little Rock in one of his periodic bouts of depression, after he broke up with his first wife. Unknown to the eight, this would be the last time they would all gather at one place. Within a year they began to scatter, with Wade first defecting to Georgia by the next fall and rarely attending subsequent agrarian meetings.

Not all sweetness and light, the meeting included some tough bargaining. Collins and the brethren had different agendas, and they pushed each other as far as possible. Collins gained a promise of complete editorial support, which meant that, ordinarily, the individual Agrarians would agree to write frequent reviews (Davidson saw this as a virtual revival of his old book page) and would offer most of their best poems and essays to Collins. On their part, the Agrarians asked for a dominant editorial role and in fact would at first be much more intimately connected to the journal than any of the other antimodernists. They also asked Collins to accept a prepared memorandum, setting forth a joint editorial or ideological position. Briefly, they stipulated that the journal would indeed advocate economic policies, but not in technical form or in isolation from their broader concerns as artists, historians, poets, and scientists. They would not be propagandists or isolate politics from a larger social and esthetic context. Rather, as critical minds, they would bring their talents to bear on economic issues so as to inform political action. At the same time, and unlike the New Humanists, they did plan to integrate economics and politics into their critical essays, while rejecting the communist bent to make material conditions the sole determinant of a culture. But, as artists, they insisted that Collins go beyond essays and opinion and publish literary criticism and the best of poems and fiction, and (Tate wanted this) at least one savage satirical article each month.

In this agreement the eight tried to clarify, as carefully as possible, religious and sectional issues. They asked for no specific religious position for the journal. They would not be prophets of any specific sect. However, religion was a special concern of Agrarians and should be of the journal. Religion was necessary for the good life, but they should not name the religion. Although this might seem equivocal, it reflected only their own lack of agreement. They noted that many antimodernists might want to certify Roman or Anglo Catholicism as the religion of the movement, and the Agrarians could see some logic in that. But they were southerners, and in the South the support for the good life had very often come from Presbyterians and Methodists or other Protestant groups, including various fundamentalists. On religion they desired only one specific editorial stance — opposition to new or soft or humanistic and naturalistic religions. As southerners they also expected contributors to the journal to respect regionalism or sectionalism, and thus a type of provincialism, and to see such as an ideal for people everywhere, for the good life had to have a specific, concrete, rooted form. They were not affirming geography, only that the quality of life embodied in the South could be realized in other regions, through regional cultures. As their final condition of joining with Collins, they asked him to publish only essays consistent with this overall philosophical outlook, a stricture he never followed.[15]

The partnership with Collins proved rocky. Within months the Agrarians were disillusioned with him. He was hard to reach, slow in responding to letters, unpredictable in his editorial policies, and, worst sin of all, derelict in paying impoverished contributors (all the Agrarians) for their reviews and essays. At one time or another every Agrarian cursed Colllins or threatened to end the relationship. But they did not, simply because they had no comparable outlet. In the next four years they served in effect as the sustaining editors of the *American Review*, collectively publishing approximately seventy reviews and essays by early 1937, or an agrarian outpouring several times more extensive than *I'll Take My Stand*. Davidson led with over twenty contributions. But by 1936 they began to back off. Only Davidson published essays in the *Review* in 1937.

They all suffered acute embarrassments when critics pointed to Collins' many pro-fascist statements, and to a sprinkling of fascist apologies that he published in the *Review*. To a large extent, the Agrarians were innocents. In April 1933, when they entered into a virtual contract with Collins, he never mentioned fascists as part of the new alliance. But by 1934 they were aware of several pro-fascist articles, which was not too surprising in a review that never adhered to any rigid ideological line. One reason for the early innocence was the ideological ferment of the depression years. Intellectuals were exploring many options, ranging from communism to Italian fascism. All seemed worthy of serious consideration. The Agrarians, often rejoicing at the breakdown of old verities, thus saw Agrarianism as a radical option, one that could gain disciples because of the debacle of the old order. In the early thirties they considered themselves rebels or revolutionaries and rather enjoyed a reputation as radicals or conspiratorial Young Turks. Thus, a fascination with what was going on in Italy, or in the Soviet Union, was normal in the America of 1933. At different times, each of the Agrarians had to give special attention to the claims of both Marxists and fascists, since both were within the pale of serious academic discussion. By 1935, however, with mounting evidence of what Hitler was doing in Germany, even Italian fascism ceased to be an intellectually respectable option among American intellectuals, just as after the end of World War II so would Soviet communism.

The Agrarians became alarmed after 1935. They faced a nasty series of accusations in 1936 from a former admirer, writer Kate Lumpkin, and tried to find an effective rebuttal. Tate was particularly worried because of his contacts and friends on the left and his sensitivity to the opinion of other writers. He recognized that his own political stance, even when he called it reactionary, shared much more with Marxists than fascists. He thought this true of all the brethren, at a time when he found the most likely agrarian support in Dorothy Day's *Catholic Worker*. The Nashville group considered a public statement repudiating Collins, which seemed ungracious for one who had befriended them in a time of great need.

Thus, after 1935, in every possible context, they repudiated both communism and fascism, or the two polar extremes to which the existing capitalistic economy would inevitably gravitate without major agrarian repairs.[16]

After the agreement with Collins, the Agrarians were off and running. In May 1933 their backed-up essays began to appear in the first number of the *American Review*. Along with a virtual barrage of agrarian articles, they quickly began planning a new book, a new and more propagandistic symposium, possibly to be out as early as the spring of 1934. In August several of the brethren again met at Lytle's farm to plan such a book. By November, Tate had a table of contents which he submitted to Harper and Brothers, with no success. In fact, during the depression, he was unable to interest any publisher in such a volume. In the tentative outline, Tate talked of a "conservative" revolution and a new, planned society, not the planned economy of social scientists (Lanier was to write against this). At least half of the proposed essays had already been published, or were about to be published, in the *American Review*. The twelve proposed authors included the eight, plus Fletcher and Nixon and, as replacements for Kline and Young, no less than T. S. Eliot and Herbert Agar, a Louisville journalist and historian, an advocate of decentralization, and a friend of Tate's. The proposed essay topics suggested their new fascination with problems of land and property ownership. Subsequent book proposals even used as a theme the "restoration of property" or as a title "The Propertied State." According to this first proposal, Ransom was to develop his ideas on land and subsistence agriculture, Warren was to write about some nineteenth-century English agrarians, including William Cobbett and John Ruskin, while they hoped Nixon would write an expert essay on the problems of landless tenants.[17]

One almost amusing effort followed the 1933 meeting with Collins. It seriously involved only Fletcher, Owsley, and Davidson, or the most fervent old Confederates among the group. Fletcher, in a visit to Nashville in 1933, had talked to Tate about a southern political movement. Out of this, he and Owsley dreamed up the idea of a new southern youth organization, which Fletcher proposed to call the Grey-Jackets. College students were to wear Confederate uniforms, fly the flag, march on stated occasions, and keep alive memories of the battles and leaders of the holy war. They were to try to destroy all movements that denied the fact of, or the glory of, the South's war for independence. Among early targets, Fletcher suggested they tear down a monument to Cyrus McCormick, whose reaper helped the North win the West and thus the war. The Grey-Jackets could threaten chambers of commerce and devise their own harvest festivals. Of course, the youth might fall into rowdyism and end up shooting blacks. Fletcher had no animus against blacks and wanted to help them gain land ownership; he even saw no reason why they could not eventually organize black Grey-Jackets, since the object was to throw the North out, not keep blacks down.

No one ever took up all these Fletcher proposals. But Davidson and Owsley had helped reconsecrate the Franklin battlefield in 1933, and at Vanderbilt they were able to organize a small, pro-southern student organization, called the Phalanx, in the second semester of 1934. Owsley said the students would have an agrarian creed, sponsor debates and forums, and each student member was to carry out a reading program on southern history and on the war and reconstruction, plus reading *I'll Take My Stand* and all the new essays in the *American Review*. They could help "renew the spirit of self-respect of the South," a subject about which Owsley confessed his emotionalism: "The angels must weep at the arrogance, complacency, conceit, and success of the Northern Intellectuals. I am bitter to the marrow, clear through the marrow. So bitter that I feel that I am losing my poise as a historian." The new club paralleled a local radio talk by Owsley on communist subversion among Negroes. The new club was largely secret, with around twenty-five members. Owsley hoped it would air issues suppressed by the carpetbag and scalawag press. Even though Davidson said the club was creating a sensation on campus, it seemed too weak to survive the one semester and, as far as Vanderbilt records indicate, expired by June 1934.[18]

The Collins agreement cemented a working alliance between the Southern Agrarians and the English Distributists. Soon they shared the same general platform, with the Agrarians applying it to the specific problems of the south. The small Distributist movement originated in the work of Hilaire Belloc, who published his opening manifesto, *The Servile State,* in 1911. By the 1930s he had gained a considerable following in England, with an organized movement and a small journal. Collins recruited an aging Belloc for the first numbers of the *American Review,* publishing in six installments what amounted to a book, "The Restoration of Property." In England, Belloc had long advocated the restoration of a rooted and stable English peasantry as an antidote to an otherwise inevitable socialist or fascist form of totalitarianism. He had also advocated a series of state initiatives, including carefully targeted taxes, to foster and protect not only family-owned farms but small manufacturers and retail shops. Such a crucial state role was necessary because open competition insured the eventual ascendancy of larger and larger firms, as Marxists argued. Obviously, by property Belloc meant not consumer goods or investment paper but the means of production—land and tools. Only a secure access to these allowed people to escape servile dependency, to gain independence and freedom, even the freedom requisite to responsible citizenship.[19]

The southern Agrarians welcomed such a point of view. It coincided neatly with Ransom's support of an agrarian agriculture. Tate soon read *The Servile State* and proclaimed property restoration as a return to a traditional American ideal. In an essay first published in the *American Review,* Tate tried to disabuse Americans of their corrupted uses of the word "property." Much influenced, as was Ransom, by Adolf A. Berle, Jr., and Gardiner C. Means's landmark 1932 book, *The Modern Corporation and Private Property,* he demonstrated the widespread and increasing separation of paper claims on profits from managerial responsibility. For Tate, any ownership apart from management, from a personal and moral responsibility for the use of capital, did not qualify as property. From the same perspective, Ransom referred to modern investors as economic geldings, emasculated and irresponsible owners with no effective control over what happened to their so-called property. And corporate managers, like overseers on antebellum southern plantations, did not own land and capital and had no personal responsibility for its humane use and no paternal regard for workers. As powerful but irresponsible hirelings, they served only two urgent goals—maximizing the profits of owners and protecting or increasing their own salaries and power.[20]

This understanding of a corporate or collective economy clarified some earlier goals of the Agrarians. In *I'll Take My Stand,* they had tried to preserve the remnants of a proprietary society, a society everywhere threatened but still dominant in agriculture. But farmers, particularly those in the South, suffered from deep maladies, some rooted in national policy, some in their own capitulation to the values of an industrial order. Thus, as one task, the Agrarians now had to try to find solutions to the economic disabilities of farmers in the depression thirties. Beyond this, they all soon joined Ransom in trying to motivate farmers to turn, at least in part, away from commercial, commodity production, away from their vulnerability to competitive prices, and back far enough toward self-providence as to bring market production in line with demand. Finally, for the economy as a whole, the Agrarians soon joined in antimonopoly crusades, in attacks on concentrated wealth, in support of vigorous antitrust enforcement, and in celebration of local handicrafts and folk arts. They joined Distributists in seeking discriminatory taxes against great wealth, or in any measures that would help decentralize production and bring it back as close as possible to the household or proprietary ideal, even if such meant some loss in efficiency.

Of the eight Agrarians who wrote for *American Review,* only Owsley was well enough informed about the maladies of southern agriculture to suggest comprehensive remedies. He began to work on a reform program acceptable to all the Agrarians, submitted ideas during 1934 to the brethren, and with their general endorsement published the results in the *American Review* in 1935 as "The Pillars of Agrarianism." This was the closest the group ever came to endorsing specific remedies for agricultural distress in the South. It included a clear endorsement of land reform and was truly agrarian in the sense of proposed limitations on acreage and new means of opening access to land. The proposals, close to ideas that Nixon and Owsley had frequently discussed, reflected their mutual concern over the evils of sharecropping and tenancy. Owsley distributed the essay widely among politicians. Senator John Bankhead of Alabama acknowledged it and applauded its recommendations. In such a small way it may have helped promote the 1936 Bankhead-Jones Farm Tenancy Act, which provided loans enabling a few worthy tenants to purchase their land.

In his first pillar, Owsley offered political schemes to rehabilitate southern agriculture, using as a model the Scandinavian countries. To a large extent he embraced New Deal agricultural programs, including easier credit and price supports. Beyond this, he urged a tenant purchase plan. He also wanted federal and state governments to buy up all bank- and absentee-owned land or excessive acreage owned by planters and use this for a new homestead program for those with farming skills (eighty acres, a log house, two mules and two cows, and living expenses for the first year). Consistent with traditional agrarian principles, these homesteads were to be unalienable, neither saleable nor mortgageable. He also endorsed laws that would prevent land speculation. For the urban employee without agricultural skills or for low-skilled blacks, he proposed apprenticeship programs on larger plantations. He also advocated special soil conservation and rehabilitation programs, with stringent penalties for private abuses of the land. He wanted to encourage more subsistence farming to control market surpluses and asked for special subsidies to farmers to balance the tariff protection or monopolistic market control enjoyed by the manufacturing and commercial sectors. Finally, in the least plausible proposal, but by now necessary to encompass the regionalism of Donald Davidson, he proposed a constitutional amendment that would divide the United States into economically rational regions, each with its own government and each with protective vetoes over threatening federal policies, a scheme reminiscent of some 1850 strategies of John C. Calhoun.[21]

Except for their writing, the Agrarians had almost no means of getting support for such agrarian reforms. As far as the records indicate, they used organizational tactics only twice. In 1935 the first Conference of Southern Policy Groups met in Atlanta. It reflected the work, and in a sense the entrepreneurship, of a Virginian and former official in the Foreign Policy Association, Francis Pickens Miller, who visited several southern cities, either speaking to or helping form local policy discussion groups. Several Agrarians were involved in such a group in Nashville. All such groups were invited to send delegates to the Atlanta meeting. Davidson and Owsley represented Nashville. Davidson read a position paper written by Owsley, and closely modeled on his "Pillars" article, but the two also

Frank Owsley (Photo by Stearn & Sons)

submitted a theoretical paper on Agrarianism. The delegates voted to organize a permanent Southern Policy Committee and elected Herman Clarence Nixon as its chairman, a post he would hold for two years. The one issue that united the deeply divided delegates was support for a tenant purchase bill then before Congress.

The Atlanta meeting made clear the ideological confusions of the mid-thirties and the uselessness of such conventional labels as liberal and conservative. In several senses, Davidson and Owsley were the radicals present, since they had a coherent and drastic proposal. To the delegates, land repurchase, free homesteads, and several policies to protect individual ownership seemed not only backward-looking but also dangerous because of the structural economic changes envisioned. The very confidence—or dogmatic certainty—of the Agrarians helped create factions and divisions. They played much the same role as Communists in other gatherings of professors, journalists, and politicians in the thirties. No wonder one delegate moved a resolution of censure (unsuccessful) against Owsley and Davidson.

This meeting also marked a still friendly but sad break between the Nashville Agrarians and Nixon. In the discussions and votes Nixon almost always sided with the majority, not the Agrarians. This reflected his developing sympathies with collectivist, or at least cooperative, efforts to solve the problems of depression-era America as well as his continued, fervent support of more ambitious New Deal measures. In the preceding three years his increasingly political activism led him into several causes that at least alarmed his Nashville friends. He had helped organize a Consumers' League in Louisiana, was sympathetic with labor unions' efforts to organize southern workers, and had avidly supported cooperative farming experiments and subsistence homesteading. He was a close friend of Will Alexander, a racial activist and Deputy Administrator of the new Resettlement Administration. He had been a member of the Southern Regional Committee, a research wing of Howard Odum's regional studies at the University of North Carolina. None of these activities clearly conflicted with Agrarianism. Owsley subsequently won a research grant from the Southern Regional Committee. But Nixon's friends, the new networks he was forming, involved largely those who identified themselves as liberals or progressives, and thus people who, at the drop of a hat, would advocate collectivist answers or who would emphasize class conflict instead of sectional exploitation. Davidson did not trust these people.

The overt break came the next year. Nixon began joining reform efforts that seemed dangerously radical to southerners. He soon cooperated with a sprinkling of Communist Party members, those who joined activist causes that Nixon saw as righteous. His often courageous activism hurt him academically and at least contributed to a controversial resignation of his professorship at Tulane in 1938, which in turn enabled him to become secretary of the new and controversial Southern Conference on Human Welfare. By then, his old agrarian buddies dismissed him as hopelessly pink, but they still liked him personally and at least kept contact. Before the second Southern Policy Conference in Chattanooga in May 1936, Nixon tried to turn the organization into an activist organization, with limited success. But one policy which he pushed—admission of a Negro to his Southern Policy Committee—led to a determined protest from James Muir Waller, a Nashville attorney and another local convert to Agrarianism. After this, Nixon struggled to gain changes in Agricultural Adjustment Administration payments to farmers, changes that would protect the rights of tenants, particularly black tenants. He sought such changes in order to avert the violence that had already erupted in Arkansas during a tenant strike backed by a new, militant Southern Tenant Farmer's Union. He came to the Chattanooga meeting with hopes of building broader support for a range of needed reforms in the South. He largely failed, for the delegates could not agree on several crucial proposals. Once again, almost all supported a tenant purchase program but only after extended debate approved a statement, largely drafted by Nixon, on a broad social security program for farmers.

Tate and Warren represented the Nashville Policy Committee at Chattanooga. They were joined by Herbert Agar of Louisville, by then coeditor with Tate of the forthcoming Agrarian-Distributist symposium, *Who Owns America?* Notably, these were more cosmopolitan, less dogmatic, delegates than Davidson and Owsley the year before. But they came to support the Agrarian-Distributist pro-

gram, with property restoration their highest priority. Tate proved
an eloquent spokesman and used every occasion to attack collectivist remedies. Accusing the Conference of moving toward such leftist, Communist-influenced groups as the Southern Tenant Farmer's
Union, Tate received plenty of abuse from some delegates. He even
provoked a motion to purge the Agrarians. Yet, he helped prevent
a collectivist victory and came back to Nashville full of enthusiasm,
believing that in one more year the Agrarians could capture the Conference. He sensed that even the North Carolina crowd was moving
their way and noted supporting votes from William C. Couch, then
Director of the University of North Carolina Press. Davidson did
not share this optimism. He was a bit leery of Tate's alliance with
Agar and Distributists and frightened by the labor-Negro sympathies revealed in the Southern Policy Conference. He shortly thereafter wrote a scathing indictment of the nonrepresentative character
of the Chattanooga meeting, noting the absence of farmers, villagers, or businessmen from the endless discussions by professors,
journalists, New Deal bureaucrats, and labor union leaders. The
Southern Policy Committee survived, but within the next year Nixon
resigned his chairmanship for more radical and activist causes, the
Committee returned to its original purpose—discussion—and the
Agrarians all but disbanded.[22]

A much more intense fratricidal dispute also came to a head in
1935, a dispute which completely severed Fletcher from the agrarian
movement. One has to pity Fletcher. All along he had considered
himself a loyal Agrarian, supporting the group from a distance. He
had eagerly endorsed every new proposal from Nashville and badly
wanted to contribute to a new symposium. His mental problems,
and erratic and unpredictable stands on issues, alarmed the Nashville group even by 1933, when he briefly lapsed into one of his in-
capacitating bouts of depression. Fletcher allowed no labels. In the
early thirties, and in an article in the *American Review,* he seemed
to move far to the right, endorsing an established church and even
the restoration of monarchy. In 1934 he even obliquely attacked
Jews. Yet, when black and white sharecroppers organized and struck
landowners in Arkansas in 1935, Fletcher rallied to their cause and,
for a time, even taught a course at socialist Commonwealth Col-

lege. In 1935, his former inheritance exhausted and his mental state once again precarious, he decided to take a stand on principle, and by so doing lost the respect of all the Agrarians save Davidson and, possibly, Owsley.

The blowup was, in part, a setup by Davidson. In early 1934 the *Virginia Quarterly Review* carried an essay by Mencken in which he unmercifully ridiculed the Agrarians, with some pointed references to Davidson. With full expectation that the editor would not publish it, Davidson wrote as a response a historical essay, one he published subsequently in the *American Review* as "I'll Take My Stand, A History."[23] Fletcher, by now a close friend of Davidson's, was incensed at Mencken's essay, an overreaction on his part to a rather typical literary battle. When he learned from Davidson that the editor of the *Virginia Quarterly,* Lambert Davis, citing too many Agrarian essays already, had rejected Davidson's article, Fletcher exploded. Davidson, who had set up Davis, rather enjoyed the moral advantage he gained. But Davidson was also ultrasensitive, and deep down he was hurt by the attack and by the rejection; thus, typically, he had turned to Fletcher and others for sympathy and support.

Meanwhile, Davis had been planning a special edition of the *Virginia Quarterly Review* on southern literature and had successfully solicited essays from Ransom, Tate, and Warren. Only belatedly and during the controversy did he solicit an essay from Davidson. Enraged over this treatment of his friend, Fletcher fired off telegrams to the three agrarian contributors, demanding that they defend Davidson's honor by withdrawing their essays and boycotting the *Virginia Quarterly.* They each refused, although they gladly supported Davidson's position in his literary battle with Davis. They had made a firm commitment to the journal and it was too late to withdraw honorably. They also understood the game between Davidson and Davis and could not identify any great principles at stake. Their response infuriated Fletcher. He wrote a flaming letter to Davidson: "*I do not propose to allow this sort of thing to go on.* The time has come for a showdown. Either Ransom and Tate are CONTRIBUTORS TO THE VIRGINIA QUARTERLY, in which case they are NOT AGRARIANS; or else they are NOT CONTRIBUTORS, in which case

I am still an agrarian." He was sick to the death of Ransom's and Tate's dallying. Davidson tried to explain, to calm him down, but to no avail.

Fletcher received a pleasant response from Warren, but one in which he affirmed his literary independence. From Tate and Ransom he received more curt replies, in effect that it was not the burden of Fletcher to arbitrate their literary decisions. Ransom prepared, but did not send, an even more devastating letter. Thus, Fletcher reaffirmed his resignation from the group and would not withdraw it. Davidson, embarrassed, defended his colleagues. But deep down he felt betrayed—perhaps an early warning sign of his alienation from Ransom and even from Tate. Fletcher kept up the battle. Warren, who had moved to Louisiana State University the fall before, planned a major literary conference in April 1935, to help launch what became the prestigious *Southern Review.* He invited all his friends, including Fletcher. Too bad. Now almost a madman, Fletcher begged a ride down to Baton Rouge with Tate and at the conference made a fool of himself on the platform, with a vicious attack on poor Davis. He rode back to Memphis with Tate, but after the Vanderbilt group left him he collapsed and had to call his sister in Little Rock to come and bring him home. He was quickly into an asylum.[24]

The Agrarians took Fletcher at his word. He was no longer included in their circle and was not asked to contribute to the 1936 symposium, *Who Owns America?* In a sense, this might have seemed a cruel response to a sick man. It was not. Fletcher recovered, won the Pulitzer Prize for selected poems in 1938, and wrote excellent local history in his later years. He remarried, carried on a warm correspondence with Davidson, and soon regretted his earlier behavior. Ransom and Tate could forgive this, but they correctly feared what he might write or say. He was too much of a risk. Fletcher's later years were generally peaceful, but sad. He felt alone, easily fell into paranoia, and flirted constantly with insanity. In his old age he desperately held on to a few friends, with Davidson perhaps closest of all. After many entreaties, Davidson and Teresa visited the Fletchers in Little Rock in April 1950. The two aging men, burdened spirits both, had a wonderful time charting the inanities of the modern world and parted with promises of future visits. Yet, within a month Fletcher, cursed almost daily by depression, got up early,

Caroline Gordon and Allen Tate in the last years of their marriage (Photo
by Ralph Morrisey)

walked to a nearby lake, and drowned, an apparent suicide. Davidson, who referred to him as a rootless exile come home, wrote a
loving memorial for *Poetry*.[25]

Throughout 1934 and most of 1935, Davidson in particular worked
at the long-deferred symposium. He compiled several tables of content, but by year's end had almost given up. No publisher would
offer a contract, and no one, as yet, had written a single essay. By
the fall of 1935, a restless Tate decided to take over the project. He
felt that Davidson and Ransom would flounder on for years. Sensitive to the wishes of publishers, he thus joined with his now close
friend, Herbert Agar, to edit an Agrarian-Distributist book. Agar,
after a best-selling history, *The People's Choice* (1931), was a major
lure for publishers. So was their plan to attack monopoly ownership, a theme much debated in the mid-thirties.

The planning of what became *Who Owns America?* took place
in the summer of 1935. The Tates had spent the previous academic
year at Southwestern at Memphis (an academic necessity, for he had
to get money to live on) but reoccupied Benfolly in the early summer, only to be flooded with endless guests. In part to escape the
crunch, in part to earn more money, the Tates left for a creative writing school in Michigan in July, only to learn at Louisville that it had
been cancelled. They undoubtedly talked at this point with Agar,
then fled south to Cornsilk (living was cheap there), then back to
Louisville to visit Agar and to plan the book, then back to Cornsilk, and only finally to Benfolly before returning to Memphis in
the fall. Agar came down to Benfolly, and Lanier and Lytle came
up from Nashville. The four did the final planning for the book and
soon had recruited most authors. Tate did not invite the other Agrarians to this planning session. He knew that the whole group would
not be able to agree; the defensive provincials such as Owsley and
Davidson would resent Agar and be jealous of an effort that undercut the long-planned and exclusively Agrarian sequel to *I'll Take
My Stand*. But Tate rather easily procured a contract from Houghton Mifflin and then used all the tact he could muster to get all the
brethren to contribute. Though Owsley and Davidson were piqued,
wary of Agar, they were won over by flattering letters from both
Agar and Tate, who argued that their contributions were essential
to the final product.[26]

Tate and Agar rushed the book. It came out in the summer of
1936 without even an index. They wanted it to precede the 1936 elec-
tion. They saw it as a type of endorsement for President Roosevelt
and, at the same time, a means of influencing the direction of the
campaign and a second Roosevelt administration. The book contained twenty relatively brief essays, including eight by the still active Agrarians; one by their Nashville friend, James Waller; another
by a near-disciple of Davidson and a fellow poet, George Marion
O'Donnell; and another by Cleanth Brooks, a former Vanderbilt
student and colleague of Warren's at Louisiana State University.
Counting all these essays, the Agrarians dominated the book. Hilaire Belloc, the guru of Distributism, graced the book with a con-
cluding essay. The other essays reflected either Distributist or conservative Catholic influences and included one essay by a woman.
H. C. Nixon turned down several pleas to contribute—he was too
busy fighting tenancy, had a greater concern for rural cooperatives
than for property, decried reactionary elements in the South, and
wanted to push Roosevelt faster towards social and economic democracy. He noted that some of his enemies called him "pink." Because
of the diversity of contributors and the lack of any common platform, the book lacked not only the verve and bite of *I'll Take My
Stand* but much of its eloquence. It received few reviews and provoked almost no controversy.[27]

The several essays by Agrarians, if anything, helped strip the
book of any clear focus. The brethren did not try to coordinate
their essays and, by 1936, possibly could not agree enough to have
done so. Lanier's scholarly analysis of business concentration, his
proposals for increased regulation and in rare cases public ownership, supported the title of the book but did little to reflect traditional Agrarian beliefs. Warren wrote a delightful but not very self-
revealing contrast of proletarian and regional writers, with a verdict
clearly favoring the Agrarians or regionalists. Wade wrote a brief,
poetic note on the endless war between city and village, with his
blessings to the village. Davidson offered another eloquent plea for
regional autonomy. Lytle, with echoes of "The Hind Tit," defended
what he called the "livelihood farm" as the backbone of any modern state. Owsley rehearsed again his indictment of the devil Hamilton and all his legacies. Tate, republishing an essay from the *Ameri-*

can Review, most clearly and forcefully supported a redistribution of property.[28]

Ransom's essay was most revealing and most clearly reflected a break from earlier Agrarianism. In one of his last detours from literary criticism into the treacherous area of public advocacy, he wrote eloquently about the problems of farmers, promoting relief in rather orthodox New Deal terms (subsidies, better schools, and cheap, TVA-like electricity). Such aid might enable more farmers to remain on the land. But, in any case, many southerners would remain employees, for some production required the efficiency of factories. For such employees he also recommended standard New Deal remedies — bargaining power for unions, unemployment insurance, improved housing, medical care, good schools, and, most intriguing, workplace rules that would accommodate the naturally slower tempo of southern life, rules that he also advocated for the North as a means of reducing unemployment. Tate had also grudgingly admitted the necessities of some factories, but he argued that workers should be able to dictate what they produced.[29]

Even as individual Agrarians began to move off in different directions, they failed in efforts to create a broader Agrarian-Distributist movement. The publication of *Who Owns America?* paralleled organizational efforts by a combined group of largely northern Distributists or back-to-the-land advocates and the Nashville Agrarians. Some of the authors met informally and socially in Nashville on 1 May to celebrate the book's publication and to plan for a major Distributist-Agrarian conference on 4–5 June. The conference was the high-water mark of cooperation. Approximately twenty-six rather diverse people gathered in Nashville to form an Alliance of Agrarian and Distributist Groups. Wade, although listed as attending, had begged off just before the meeting, thus preventing a final gathering of the remaining Agrarians, but Cleanth Brooks, O'Donnell, and James Waller did come, making ten Agrarians, or not quite half of a motley group, which included Ralph Borsodi (an avowedly rationalist or secularist decentralist), several Catholic priests or laymen, a small sprinkling of college professors, and Agar. Lanier served as elected chairman, with business sessions during the first day, an open meeting in the evening, and committee reports the second day. The Alliance, on its subsequent stationery, listed the one common concern of the group: "We advocate the wide-spread ownership of land and other productive property. We deplore the disappearance of the private owner under monopoly-capitalism, communism, and fascism."[30]

On the second day, a committee on a platform, chaired by Agar but including Ransom, reported to the group. It proclaimed liberty endangered, and asked for new social and educational institutions to save it. In a just society, power has to be dispersed among citizens, who have to be free from outside control. Only a wide distribution, and responsible ownership, of property could assure such liberty. The proclaimed enemies of such freedom were finance capitalism (monopoly and regimentation), communism (violent methods and regimentation), and fascism (violence, regimentation, and a nationalist state). The platform recognized the primacy of agriculture, celebrated new inventions but not when used in factories, talked of a needed decentralization of people, and asked for public ownership of or control over natural monopolies. For large, necessarily private firms, it asked protection for employees, union bargaining rights, and opportunities for workers to become owners.[31]

Other committees recommended a formal organization. The group planned to meet again the following spring, set up a Secretariat with offices both in Nashville and New York City, and proposed a new magazine (Tate chaired this committee) tentatively called *New America*. But the dream soon faded. The groups were not able to continue a working alliance. Jealousies existed even at the organizing meeting. Owsley and Davidson were leery of some aspects of the platform and of cooperation with some of the people who attended the meeting. In early December, Ransom noted that Agar and the New York group were ready to go ahead with the magazine, while the Agrarians wanted more time. He, Lytle, and Lanier agreed to let the New York crowd do it without their help, leaving them free to start their own agrarian journal. At Christmas-time disillusioned Agrarians gathered and talked mournfully about the end of any joint movement or even about the end of Agrarianism. From all these conversations, Ransom drew the necessary conclusions and communicated them by letter to one of the Distributists in January 1937. He explained why the Agrarians could not commit themselves to a planned spring conference. He noted that the one

cooperative venture had failed (the magazine) and that the eastern-
ers were too close to the cooperative movement, too sympathetic
to single taxers, and too open to liberal Christianity to please all
the Nashville group. Thus, if the Agrarians agreed to a joint meeting, they would suffer conspicuous defections at home. Ransom accordingly suggested, after extensive talks with the brethren, that
they give up on any working alliance and part as good friends.[32]

The resulting magazine, *Free America,* never became even an outlet for the Agrarians. Davidson published two short articles, in 1938
and again in 1939, while Tate very briefly assumed the literary editorship in 1930–1940, during which period Davidson wrote one
book review. But the small magazine very soon became a guidebook
for modern homesteading, with Ralph Borsodi gaining a dominant
voice. It was innocuous enough, not at all dangerous, almost an
early version of *Organic Gardening.* This is why Davidson did not
hesitate to make contributions. But Tate had larger philosophical
goals to pursue and ended the last Agrarian support early in 1940.
Long before this, the Southern Agrarians were in disarray and in
retreat, not primarily because of the failure of the alliance but because of internal differences and Ransom's lagging zeal.

V.

In Retreat

It all began to fall apart in 1937. The agrarian movement had reached a dead end. It had no place to go. From now on even the three who remained most loyal to at least some version of Agrarianism (Davidson, Lytle, Owsley) talked in the past tense, about what had been. Nostalgic memories replaced political action. Even for these three, Agrarianism became the second lost cause.

The failed alliance with the Distributists was not a cause but a symptom of agrarian retreat. One problem was physical dispersion. Until 1934 eight continuing Agrarians all had a tie to Vanderbilt or to Nashville. The propinquity, the fellowship, bound the group together. In 1934 Wade returned to Georgia, Warren moved to Louisiana State University, and Tate spent the academic year in Memphis. But zeal and new challenges kept the wayward on board through 1936. By then, neither Wade nor Warren had the commitment for any continued, time-consuming agrarian efforts, and slowly, without any conversion or any announcement, withdrew emotionally from the magical circle. Lanier, most open to larger alliances, gifted with organizational skills, but an infrequent contributor to the literary battles, lost in a major faculty fight at Vanderbilt in 1936–37, and in 1938 moved to a new, and much more lofty, academic position at Vassar.

Much more critical was the scattering of Tate and Ransom, which left only Davidson, of the big three, in Nashville. The Tates, without realizing it at the time, spent their last summer at Benfolly in 1937. That fall Tate took a nontenured position at the University of North Carolina Women's College at Greensboro, and from there would move on to Princeton. Financial need kept Tate working even summers and made any return to Benfolly impossible. In 1946 he sold it. He never defected. He continued to affirm his agrarian philosophy until his death. But from 1937 on he supported it only through his literary criticism. He could justify this by his claim, one made even before 1937, that he never considered Agrarianism a political movement with achievable goals, a view that saddened Davidson. Instead, it had always been a philosophical, ultimately a religious crusade, with the South, and even agrarian themes, simply ways of exemplifying the underlying principles. With increasing bitterness, Tate saw these principles as minority ones, bound to be swamped by the perverse course of modern history. Thus, he used criticism as another way of championing his lost cause, and as time went on came to view Agrarianism as largely a type of religious affirmation.[1]

More threatening to any continued movement was the more open defection of Ransom. He had been the leader, philosopher, and balance wheel of the group. By the end of 1936 he was tired of, disillusioned with, Agrarianism. He began another reorientation of his life and in 1937 moved to small Kenyon College in Ohio. His defection stripped the heart out of the agrarian cause. Behind his choices lay both philosophical and academic concerns.

Ransom, with his usual degree of detachment, recognized by late 1936 that the Agrarians had no place to go. In 1928 they had joined in a cultural game played by almost all intellectuals—criticizing the spiritual agonies of a new, collectivized, dependency-creating economy. Ransom never repudiated this criticism, although he came to understand how precious and indulgent it could be, how far removed from the concrete concerns of people caught up in, or victimized by, the great depression.

In the early thirties, as the old order seemed to break apart, it had been easay for intellectuals to plot dramatic new policy options. Many played this political game. But by 1937 it was clear that radical options, whether they involved a politicization of a collective economy through some form of socialism or restoration of property and decentralized, more personalized forms of production, had not gained any but minority support in America. And, from all the evidence, socialist remedies had more appeal than schemes for restoring proprietorship. Americans had opted for a mild, middle way, one epitomized by new regulatory agencies and several new welfare programs. The Agrarians had all along dismissed as superficial and inadequate such mild repairs to the existing industrial system. But by 1937 Ransom was willing to accept them, not as ideal answers but as the only realizable ones. They made industrialism bearable from his perspective, not from that of Tate and Davidson.

The Agrarians, when they moved from a critique of what they called industrialism to a positive program, risked defeat. They also risked confusion, and by 1937 confusion was more evident than any clear program. Despite the seeming implications of their forceful essays, none of the Agrarians had ever proposed, seriously or in detail, any major dismantling of existing factories. They did propose strong antimonopoly laws and the breakup of monopolistic firms (not a new or daring proposal, to say the least). For the South, they had wanted to slow, or stop, the shift from family farms or small shops to factory production but never proposed to tear down existing southern factories. In 1933 and 1934 they believed, with a degree of satisfaction, that some closed mills would not reopen, and thus Ransom's proposal for a modest return to the land and to more subsistence agriculture. At best, these shifts would have affected no more than 20 percent of the work force, leaving the other 80 percent virtually as before.

What about them? Ransom and most of his Distributist allies had two answers—government ownership of natural monopolies or very large, monopolistic industries and, for all the rest, simply more regulation and more welfare. Thus, beyond the limits of decentralizing and restorative policies, indeed their highest priority, they lined up with, or even to the left of, the New Deal. In any case, as Herbert Agar admitted, they at least supported a major, even if ultimately self-liquidating, increase in the power of the central government, the leviathan so feared by Davidson. The only consoling hope was that, in time, with the breakup of large firms, the restored competition among equals would allow a shrinking of governmental authority, or a slight twist on Marxist visions of a first stage of detailed government regulation followed by informal, noncoercive, nonstate forms of control. Not only Davidson, but Lytle and even Owsley, feared the noneconomic implications of such federal power. Race was always on their mind. Thus, as Ransom had to admit in January 1937, in announcing the divorce of Agrarians and Distributists, the policies of the northern group were already such as to force defections in Nashville.

But what practical option did the Agrarians have? Even the Distributist program, after 1938, seemed quaint and eccentric. It is not surprising that it quickly shrank into a minor back-to-the-farm, back-to-the-household movement, one that has had moments of appeal and one that has survived on the fringes of reform in America. More aggressive efforts to break up large firms or to restore individual property seemed completely unrealistic after 1938, as unrealistic as Davidson's Calhoun-like proposal for basic constitutional changes to give regions a protective veto over federal policies. Such an aggressive regionalism would have undercut the regulatory, welfare, and limited nationalization goals of the Distributists. Thus, for Davidson, Lytle, and Owsley the only option, and one that they gradually embraced, was a cranky, increasingly paranoid, defense of the South against the North or, in reality, against the federal government, which in their estimation had once again become the aggressive tool of the North in a second reconstruction. For a time they balanced this with continued and quite radical proposals to aid southern farmers. But in World War II, with race moving to the foreground, they slowly, at times self-consciously, dropped almost all their economic demands and became angry participants in a type of cultural politics keyed closely to race. Such a defensive provincialism, although it had broad southern appeal up through the fifties, soon seemed even more eccentric and blind than modern homesteading, as well as morally obtuse, and proved in time to be much more ephemeral in its appeal.

Ransom believed that the only realistic tactic for Agrarians was practical or political surrender. He was consoled that what he called American industrialism, regulated and stripped of its worse abuses, was at least bearable even if not comely. Its vulgar side, its alienating potential, remained, but in America it at least allowed sensitive dissenters like Ransom the freedom to criticize it, and to gather in nice, insulated enclaves of good taste and noncommercial values. Artists and writers had to make their peace with the system and could do so as long as they retained such artistic freedom and such personal avenues of escape. In fact, not only did a business civilization allow such gardens of reflection, such a minority and essentially subversive culture as that of liberal arts colleges, but it often generously supported such enclaves. Ransom was soon involved in successful fund-raising for his new enthusiasm, the *Kenyon Review.* Thus, as he confessed to Tate, by 1937 he had decided to retreat back to literature and to give up on economics and politics. In a sense he had been burned and was now disillusioned. In fact, he would soon chart the multiple illusions, the misplaced hopes of the earlier agrarian crusade.[2]

At Kenyon, Ransom cultivated art and religion as a type of ironic retreat from the fury of practical life, a retreat not necessary in formerly more holistic agrarian economies. By 1945 he concluded that freedom, leisure, and brotherly love remained possible in artistic enclaves, among the few who attained a type of salvation through retreat. There was no other answer, no way back to the old society. Besides, as he confessed, no one would like the old ways, for who could give up science, productive tools, and the human comforts they allow, or the scholarship that they subsidize? The arts are a beautiful expiation, worth the sick welter through which homeless spirits must wander between times (he had been reading Santayana). Intellectuals, not without guilt, had to go along with the existing economy. As confessed sinners, they knew that they had lost their earlier innocence. By then he saw the Southern Agrarians as futile seekers after such a lost innocence. Yet, they did not really go back to the farm (actually, in addition to such real, if often leisurely farmers as Lytle, Nixon, and Wade, Ransom in 1933 had moved out to a subsistence farm south of Nashville, Owsley in 1935 had purchased a farm at White's Creek, and most Agrarians at least dabbled in gardening). But could they, in good faith, invite others, including their "business friends," to do what they never really did— take up farming as a career? And could they try to confine existing farmers to their "gardens of innocence"? Thus, to the despair of Davidson, Ransom saluted the earlier, innocent "agrarian nostalgia" as a valuable way of celebrating a proper human economy and applauded the Agrarians for defending the freedom of the arts, whose function they did understand, much better than did the modern exponents of economic progress. In Davidson's view, Ransom had simply joined the enemy, an enemy Davidson now variously described as hated industrialists or as liberals and progressives.[3]

Ransom's disaffection had more than political realism behind it. It was his way of coping with an impossible academic situation at Vanderbilt. From 1934 to 1937 all the Agrarians at Vanderbilt became disaffected with University policies. They all became leaders in an antiadministration faction within the faculty. The tensions went way back, at least for an embittered Tate. Tate never trusted either an unbearably conventional Edwin Mims or Chancellor Kirkland and liked to take verbal potshots at them at any opportunity. Then, from 1931 to 1934, Warren had gained only a demeaning and temporary instructorship at Vanderbilt and felt the normal insecurity of such a position. From Mims's perspective, it seemed he was bending over backwards to find for Warren work and a meager income. Though Warren was, at times, appreciative, he was also bitter at being in a position of having practically to beg for his living. Even this job evaporated in 1934, perhaps to Warren's advantage. He sought and gained a permanent position at Louisiana State University. But Tate felt that his protégé had been treated horribly and ever after lambasted the University for getting rid of "Red." Owsley had several run-ins with Kirkland, failed to gain the chair in History, and by 1935 looked forward, possibly more than anyone else at Vanderbilt, to the early retirement of an old, inflexible chancellor who indeed had stayed on at least ten years beyond normal retirement. By then, all the Agrarians felt unappreciated or resented by the central administration at Vanderbilt.

The climax came in the spring semester of 1937. In 1935, Oliver C. Carmichael, an Alabama educator, came to Vanderbilt as Dean of Graduate Studies, and, by all acknowledgement, as the chancellor-in-waiting. He tried to build his reputation through a major and idealistic reorganization of the curriculum of the College of Arts and Science. He appointed his ablest, most prestigious faculty, including Ransom and Lanier, to a committee to propose reforms. With almost utopian zest, they prepared a complete overhaul of the curriculum, with special six-hour courses each quarter and a final, integrative course in each discipline. The plan would have required almost every professor to change existing courses or to prepare new ones. Thus, a coalition of faculty, including many old-timers, formed an opposition to the newfangled reforms, in part out of self-interest, in part because of an opposing educational philosophy. It so happened that many of the closest friends of Kirkland joined the opposition. Kirkland sympathized with their views, soon saw all the reformers as enemies, and feared that the deep divisions would prevent a smooth transition to a new chancellor. Thus, he took charge, forced new procedures and a new committee, and even in one case appealed to his Board, largely to emasculate the reforms and to prevent any semblance of faculty government at Vanderbilt. Carmichael caved in to Kirkland, deserted his faculty committee, but thereby saved his impending chancellorship.[4]

By the end of the fight, both Ransom and Lanier were Kirkland's most clearly identified enemies on campus. He so characterized them. Kirkland wanted them out of Vanderbilt. When they both chose outside opportunities, he did little to keep them. Ransom's acceptance of an offer from Kenyon College in Ohio led to a well-publicized controversy in Nashville and the South, and to acute embarrassment for Vanderbilt. The way the administration handled the offer, and how it had treated Ransom, led not only to the loss of two Agrarians, but to bitter, lasting resentment and hostility on the part of the two Vanderbilt survivors, Owsley and Davidson, who never again trusted Carmichael.

Despite the curriculum fight at Vanderbilt, Ransom might still have accepted the beguiling offer from Kenyon. There he would have lighter teaching loads, a slightly higher salary, and soon a chance to edit a major literary journal. Perhaps more important, he could escape not only all the faculty politics at Vanderbilt but also the latter-day agrarian cause, which had taken so much of his time. On 10 June 1937, after numerous petitions from colleagues and former students, he decided to accept the Kenyon offer. After all, the best Vanderbilt salary offer was $4,200; the football coach at Vanderbilt received $10,000. Tate intruded himself into the fight with a bitter letter to Kirkland, which he sent to the *Nashville Tennessean* for publication. He stressed the ability and fame of Ransom, the dimensions of the loss for southern literature, and made nasty cracks about the inability of chancellors and trustees, men of organization and finance, to evaluate the work of talented professors. After Ransom decided to go, Tate helped organize a major, and spiteful, honorary dinner, an informal affair set up as a pointed contrast to stiff and formal ceremonies marking the long-awaited event — Kirkland's retirement. Tate brought as many of his literary friends as possible to Nashville. Ford Madox Ford presided in white duck trousers and read appreciative letters from a dozen eminent writers, including T. S. Eliot, Edmund Wilson, Mark and Carl Van Doren, Carl Sandburg, Archibald MacLeish, Louis Untermeyer, and Katherine Anne Porter.[5]

By 1937, Ransom had made another drastic shift in interest and commitment, or one of those conversions that marked his career. As usual, he gave himself completely to a new cause and very suddenly dropped an old one. He told Tate, as early as December 1936, that Agrarianism was in his past. His political concerns had eaten away at his lyricism, diverted him from his literary vocation. He had "to get out of it." His new enthusiasm was an old one — literary criticism. He asked Tate to join in creating a new "objective literary standard" and forming an American Academy of Letters, all to counteract the "agrarian-distributist movement in our minds." Tate and he were to found the academy, one made up of an elite group with a traditionalist orientation (the one tie to the agrarian past). He proposed an original membership and wanted to award book prizes each year. Notably, his list of twenty-five charter members included Ransom, Tate, Wade, and Young, but not Davidson, Lytle, Owsley, or Warren (but given enough time, those rejected brethren might qualify). Soon he was as excited about these new plans as he had been in 1929 about *I'll Take My Stand*. Within a year, the *Kenyon Review* replaced his hoped-for academy and provided an outlet for two decades of productive critical writing for Ransom. He tried, for a few months, to bring Tate to Kenyon as coeditor but could not get the needed funds. Soon he and Tate shared several critical doctrines and would soon be identified as two of only four or five major architects of a new criticism.[6]

In many ways, Tate and Ransom diverged, as critics as well as persons. By his Kenyon years, Ransom had given in to his own skeptical, naturalistic bent. He had done enough homage to his Methodist origins, relieved enough guilt over an apostasy that was beyond any choice. A religious attitude remained important to him, but such an attitude required no gods and no metaphysical certainties. Religion was a natural expression of human need and human imagination. Ransom was attracted to the rich naturalism of John Dewey, who used the word *nature* to encompass matter, life, and meaning systems or mind. As a critic, Ransom tried to stay close to material and animal foundations, disliked mysticisms, exhibited an unusual degree of detachment, but could be pretentious in the use of philosophical jargon.

Tate, as he grew older, craved certainty as he moved toward conversion to Catholicism in 1950. He spent his adult career in fighting what he saw as a one-dimensional, naturalistic view of man. He wanted the unified authority of a universal Church. Much more passionate than Ransom, more moralistic but less philosophically pretentious, he wrote much more sensitive and brilliant evaluations of other writers but was never as theoretical. In his comments on critical theory, he often stated broad themes or borrowed from Ransom many of his technical insights. His depth of involvement, his integrity, was always beyond question.

The label "New Criticism" probably conceals more than it reveals about Ransom and Tate. Ransom was most responsible for the popularity of the label. He used it for one collection of critical essays. More important, he launched the *Kenyon Review* with a sense of a new beginning. To Tate he argued that literary criticism was practically a new, underdeveloped field, just waiting for new directions. As usual, he developed the sense of a new crusade with himself in the lead. He felt that his criticism could give ideas and direction to the whole profession of letters, one so badly in need of reform. He even had vague plans about capturing the Modern Language Association. At times he pushed his claims to the extreme, insisting in 1941 that his poetic theory constituted a science, a new kind of science involving a new kind of discourse.[7]

The point of agreement between Tate and Ransom was a common argument that criticism should be objective, and that art, or literature, or at least poetry constituted a type of truth. This begged some technical issues. But prior to attending these, they both insisted upon a more general point. The focus of criticism should be, in any field, entirely upon the work of art, in its wholeness and unity, in its integrity and truthfulness. The critic should try to understand and then evaluate the work of art. This meant understanding the creative purpose, the skills, and the formal conventions that guided an artist, for only then could one judge how well he or she had combined these in the completed work. This may sound truistic, but in the context they felt it almost revolutionary. For, in their judgment, most so-called literary critics had largely involved themselves with other questions—why the art came to be, what motivated the artist, what social conditions or political purposes lay behind the effort, or what moral consequences came from the art? Critics had been doing history, biography, social analysis, and moral philosophy, not artistic evaluation. In this sense the new criticism was simply an invitation to do criticism, to attend carefully to a work of art, to make it central to the critical task.

They were not extremists. They never denied the possible relevance of other disciplines, such as history and psychology, to the critical task. They only insisted that these types of knowledge not divert one from criticism, that they contribute directly to an understanding of a work of art. For example, either the historical context, or biographical insights, may enable one to understand the language of a poet. In this sense, these were necessary tools of criticism. Tate, much more than Ransom, always emphasized the moral relevance of art and saw criticism as contributing to moral ends. But each argued that moral judgment was not integral to the critical task. Moralism precluded rigorous criticism and, in a sense, impeded the moral end served by good criticism, just as premature judgments about the use of cognitive propositions may divert one from the question of their validity. Once the validity is established, then one may chart uses. The same is true for a poem. The determination of its status and achievement as a poem properly proceeds questions about its usefulness in a society. If poetry has a social value, then, presumedly, good poetry has greater value. But the judgment about its quality is clearly not a moral judgment.

The problematic claim of both Tate and Ransom was that art or, more often in their more limited context, poetry is a type of truth. Neither of them had the analytical skills to clarify all the issues begged by the claim. In 1940, Tate, with the usual excessive passion, attacked what he called the positivist or scientific approach to poetry. All such were reductionist. Historical, biological, and psychological approaches had led to the spiritual darkness of the present age. Such reductionist strategies, based on the denial of the radical discontinuity between the physical and spiritual realms, had undermined the subject matter of literature. Such approaches would, he feared, lead to the extinction of literature in a totalitarian future and its replacement by the propaganda of pressure groups in a bourgeois, mechanical, monopoly-capitalist, gadget-ridden society. In the perspective of a vulgar, utilitarian, middle-class society, poetry would be inconceivable. But, as the apocalypse approached, the duty of the critic was to point out the special, unique, and complete knowledge offered by great literature. Such knowledge was not a concealed form of social or political expression. It could not be dissolved into history or any science.

To Tate, a poem was not a substitute for, or a representation of, anything else. It had its own complete integrity. But when asked, What type of knowledge is it? Tate was always a bit elusive. He said that a successful work of art expressed a knowledge of the whole object (reminiscent of the whole horse in *I'll Take My Stand*), in its fullest objective and subjective expression. The realm of expression is its object. It does not take such an experience and reduce or dwarf it into abstract relationships. The sciences do that. Rather, to know a work of art is to grasp experience as imaginatively formed, not as reduced. It seems that the subject, in this case, is experience at a primary or original level of integration, when the abstract content is no more focal than the rich and unique qualities that are the experience, when the wholeness of the experience has not been eroded by class terms or categories.[8]

Whatever the exact content of its holistic and experiential subject matter, Tate demanded that a poem be a concise, coherent expression of it. He wanted no obscurity, no false notes. Every line, every word of a good poem should contribute to such full expression, to the most complete grasp of the whole. It should, to the limits of language, encompass both the objective and subjective facets of experience, ranging variously from the fullest extension (universality) to the fullest intensity (the most subtle nuances of individual life).

He denied any specifically poetic experience, any specifically poetic language, any prescribed emotional experience. The assumption of such had corrupted earlier poetry. All experiences are potentially its subject, even as poetry is a particular way of knowing. The experienced world is infinitely complex; so is good poetry. It takes work to create it and to understand it. It requires all our intellectual resources. Nonetheless, it is not obscure, or a matter of impressionistic reactions. Since a poem is not raw experience, but experience imaginatively formed, then critics must focus upon form. Despite accepted conventions, these forms are not fixed but themselves open to choice and thus ever-changing. This indicated his openness to "modernism" and his rejection of formal dogmatism, a dogmatism he occasionally glimpsed in Ransom's more logical theoretical essays.[9]

Ransom tried to take a tough-minded approach to criticism. He was most directly influenced by Aristotle and Kant, and by three major contemporary philosophers—John Dewey, George Santayana, and Alfred North Whitehead. Instead of repeating his earlier attacks on the empirical sciences, he now tried to give them their due. As a mode of conceptualizing and abstracting aspects of human experience, the sciences had clearly succeeded, in the practical sense of meeting many of the material needs of people. The arts, and poetry in particular, are also rooted in human experience, even in animal needs and urgencies. A person is a biological organism, nothing more. There is nothing supernatural or mysterious about the arts. When people have a secure existence, when they have enough to eat, when they have time and unexpended energy, they can move from utility, from a desire to dominate nature, to appreciation, to a love of precious objects because of their beauty, or to the creation of such objects, which is art. But the subject matter of such art is always some aspect of nature, as experienced. All these themes he borrowed from John Dewey's influential *Art as Experience.* In appreciation, and in art, nature reveals a plentitude never captured in the abstractions of science. The concreteness, the particularities, of experienced objects are at the center of art, even as they are ignored in the classifications of science. Thus, in poetry the language is very different from that in the sciences, for poets usually focus on singularities and not classes, indulge richness and deliberate ambiguity, and utilize metaphors, images, analogies, and meter and rhyme. This was a new way for Ransom to affirm what he emphasized back in Fugitive days—in art one merges the conceptual content of experience (the head) with qualitative experiences (the heart). The language of poetry is closer to the reality experienced, to the rich nuances and wholeness of any perceptual moment. Poetry is phenomenological, in the sense that it, without losing its conceptual form, its meaning, still comes close to expressing how it is to experience.

But a poem is not a recording of experience, not the babble of pure joy or undisciplined exclamation. It is a way of ordering experience, else it would not be art. A poem is a deliberate creation and, in intent, a truthful creation. It also involves learned techniques or conventions, and thus skills, as does any creation in any field. As a product of human labor, it deserves critical judgment. Did the poet do it well? Since technical skills are required, this type of critical judgment has objective reference. A critic must study the techniques, the discipline. For poetry, this means the unique formal tools, such as meter and tropes. Criticism is not history, not private impressions, not synopses or paraphrases, not linguistic analysis, not a delimiting analysis of parts taken from the whole, and not moral judgment. It is, simply, a matter of esthetic judgment. Within the conventions of the art form, did one succeed in achieving certain esthetic goals? This means that the critic has a quite technical task.[10]

In one of his most influential essays, Ransom called for an "ontological" critic. In part, he was being pretentious, parading philosophical jargon among less philosophically learned colleagues. He liked to pile on terms such as esthetic and ontology, even when he scarcely needed such heavy support or even when he failed to define the words. His point was simply that poetry has a different subject matter, points to a different reality, from the sciences. It deals with the "more refractory world of perception and memory," with the qualities of immediate experience before they are reduced to classes and categories. It must use rich, expressive words, not precise ones; attend to the natural order and rhythm of words, not their propositional logic. In some technical linguistic analysis, he characterized the signs used by scientists as symbols, abstractive by nature, and the characteristic signs of poets as icons, which point to or designate experience in its concrete wholeness. Such icons intentionally loosen up the logic of discourse, and to some extent cloud the argumentative intent of language. Poetic devices, such as meter, iconic in use and attuned to the sound of words, create a tension with the cognitive goals of clarity and precision.

Ransom refused to move beyond such necessary tension and would not allow the poet the privilege of nonsense, of words stripped of conceptual content and simply turned into musical notes. Thus, in his view, poetry always has a hybrid quality. It must do justice both to precise meaning and logical argument on one side, and to the ultimately inexpressible richness of experience on the other. In his more stilted guidelines for critics, he asked them to attend both to the determinate meaning of concepts and the indeterminate meaning introduced by formal techniques. He wanted as much clarity, as much determinate meaning, as possible in a poem, and with Tate condemned verbal tricks, emotional associations, romantic excess, or what he viewed as indulgent and sloppy writing. The icons are additive but must not detract from clear meaning in words as symbols, which all words are, to some extent. Phonic effects, although in some sense definitive of poetry, must not replace or undermine meaning, a point of view that tied Ransom to classical and rational views of poetry. When a "modern" poet allowed new techniques, or brilliant images, to confuse logic and symbolic meaning rather than add rich iconic meaning, Ransom deprecated the poet's achievement. [11]

In 1941, Ransom tried to tie criticism to Kantian thought and went further than ever again in emphasizing its scientific and objective status. In describing criticism as a form of pure speculation, he emphasized that a critic should attend purely to the art object, not its effect on people. A poem always contains a central logic or story line, and to this extent resembles prose or even a scientific essay, but it always joins this with lively local, nongeneralizable details, which are not an aspect of scientific writing. A solitary focus on the first part—on the story line or argument or sermon—easily diverts criticism into moral judgment, as reflected in Marxist criticism. The purpose, and esthetic achievement, of the artist relates primarily to the second aspect, to the local, concrete details. The formal elements of a poem, such as meter or metaphor, best fit this focus. Thus a poem may, usually does, have a moral content in its argument, but this is apart from its esthetic achievement. The gauge of this achievement is not argument, or effect, or use, but the joy gained in the immediate experience. Esthetic values are not instruments but goods in themselves, and such goods are the goal of artistic effort. Ransom refered to argumentative content plus an "X," which should not distort or diminish the logical core. But the added element gives the reader a sense of the duality of the situation, because of the experiential qualities present, and this is an added dimension. The critic should comment on both the argument or structure and the texture, the latter of which makes it a poem and not just an essay. With almost pedantic emphasis, Ransom used this structural-textural distinction in his criticism. But the textural element always, to some extent, wars against the structure or the argument, making poetry an untidy and less than rational form of discourse.[12]

As critics, Tate and Ransom had enormous influence in the field of literature. So, in a more practical, institutional context did Brooks and Warren, who in 1938 illustrated this narrowly focused, intense, analytical form of criticism in their influential text, *Understanding Poetry*. Soon this type of criticism became commonplace in English departments. But even though it derived from former Agrarians, it is not clear that it was in any necessary sense agrarian criticism. Davidson, for example, thought Ransom's prescriptions too technical and narrow, too apolitical and escapist, and never really embraced any version of the New Criticism. Thus, he believed it represented for its advocates more of a substitute for Agrarianism than a continuation.[13]

Tate disagreed. He refused to separate his criticism from his agrarian advocacy. To him, they represented complementary strategies for achieving a single goal. Whether the emphasis was on the integrity and truthfulness of a rooted and regional culture, or of a carefully crafted poem, mattered little. Both challenged the pretentious claims of abstract, reductionist science, and of a hollow industrial order based upon it. In his view, his criticism was indeed consistent with, an outgrowth of, his Agrarianism, part and parcel of a lifelong crusade he waged against materialism.

Davidson, in a lifetime of reviewing, read and criticized more books than Tate and Ransom combined. Yet he never delved deeply into any theory about criticism and was suspicious of too much logic or too many abstractions. He placed literature in a broader social context and shared a point of view with older Christians or modern Marxists. The specialized arts are part of the total culture, and each art has a social and moral role. The larger goals of a society, such as justice, have an esthetic component, and it is not a betrayal of esthetic norms, or of artistic freedom, to ask the specialized arts to contribute to these larger, more encompassing goals. That is, the artist has a responsibility to the higher arts, such as politics. He or she may, indeed, deny such responsibility, but nonetheless his or her art will have political implications and effects. Thus, in his criticism, Davidson was never content to stop with purely formal evaluations, although he conceded to Tate and Ransom the importance of internal evaluation. He saw this as a preface to larger questions that had a historical, economic, and political component. He soon dismissed Ransom as politically naive in his hope that he could somehow isolate art, or artists, from the larger problems of a society, and as morally irresponsible in seeking an Epicurean garden retreat. In a sense, such a critical perspective explained Davidson's continued dedication to political Agrarianism.

Davidson's critical interest increasingly centered on southern literature. In his last years his great consolation, his only vindication, was the flowering of that literature. He loved to chart all the names, tended to exaggerate the achievement of southern writers, and at times asserted a near southern monopoly on American literature. In the great battle of the sections, this was the only clear victory. But even it was not an unalloyed victory. Davidson, influenced by Tate, explained the flowering, not as just the normal outgrowth of a settled, conservative, religious social order, but as a defense of such an order in a time of crisis or external threat. The literary flowering reflected a new and defensive southern self-consciousness at a time when formerly assured beliefs and values were under assault. Implicit in this explanation was an ephemeral aspect to the renaissance. It would fade either if the threats evaporated, leading back toward an old South that was not very creative in the fine arts, or if the extreme enemies prevailed, destroying the social order conducive to great literature. Davidson did not probe these dilemmas, but spent most of his last years trying to keep southern writers faithful to the cause. Earlier they had too easily wandered off into sentimental, dishonest, local color writing, largely to titillate northern audiences. Now they too often capitulated to the cultural standards emanating from New York City and in various ways betrayed the South. They did this by romanticizing the Negro, by exaggeratedly emphasizing southern failures or economic deficiencies, or by endorsing capitalist, commercial, aggressive, antireligious values—values he usually labeled as progressive, liberal, or even communist. Thus, Davidson intruded ideology, tests of regional integrity and loyalty, into his judgments about southern literature, a strategy that dismayed Tate and Ransom.[14]

For Davidson, Agrarianism did not even begin to expire in 1937. He kept the faith. So did Owsley and Lytle. But the three realized that they were as voices crying in the wilderness. The brethren had scattered or defected. Of course, by the late thirties, Agrarianism had already gained disciples, including many former students. Davidson, in particular, rejoiced in these and kept contact, even creating by correspondence small circles of like-minded people. But of the original brethren, only he and Owsley remained in close contact. A younger Lytle, now married, was for a time at Monteagle, then at the University of Florida, absorbed in his own writing, and generally offered support only from a distance or on rare occasions when he visited the Vanderbilt campus. By World War II he was no longer an intimate of either Davidson or Owsley. Thus, the two of them, aging, alienated from policies at Vanderbilt, increasingly bitter critics of their society, almost gleefully chanting the steps toward a coming apocalypse, lived out the final, sad winding down of Southern Agrarianism.

Frank Owsley remained a passionate warrior until his death in 1956. By the breakup of the Agrarians in 1937, he was already involved in the arduous, pioneer scholarship that fully occupied the final phase of his career as a historian. By the laborious, detailed, statistical analysis of mass data—wills, church records, census reports, probate records, tax records, deeds, and a few private memoirs and diaries—Owsley and his graduate students developed the fullest profile ever assembled of the antebellum population of selected, representative counties in Tennessee, Georgia, Alabama, Mississippi, and Louisiana, including grain and cattle areas, lowlands and uplands, rich lands and poor. This research eventuated in a still-acclaimed book, *Plain Folk of the Old South* (1949). Although the brethren at times resented his almost complete absorption in such scholarship, they all acknowledged its direct tie to Agrarianism. Owsley's ideology at least guided him to the subject and in several ways even shaped the outcome. In the counties surveyed, small farmers, with only a few slaves or none, made up the backbone of a complex rural economy. These yeomen were not at all poor whites of myth, for they had a vital, nondeferential role in politics, were mostly literate, and set the terms of religious and cultural life. In most cases, according to Owsley's most challengeable interpretation, they lived in harmony with the few large planters. Certainly Owsley did not paint an irenic view of this antebellum South, but his emphasis upon class harmony, upon the key role of the yeoman, upon a cohesive and idealized white folk culture, upon the strengths of a diversified, self-sufficient agriculture, and upon the possibilities of social mobility gave an almost romantic, Jeffersonian patina to his story, and helped confirm his own pro-southern, anti-Yankee sentiments.[15]

Owsley managed to keep most of his private views out of his book. But not out of his letters. During the years he completed *Plain Folks,* he became personally embittered and alienated. From 1930 on, he was unhappy with the administration at Vanderbilt and frequently was tempted to take a position elsewhere. In 1932 he had referred to Edwin Mims as a "tail-wagging and belly-dragging, cur variety" son-of-a-bitch, the typical "new southerner," defeated, "conquered bastard-American." The South was in the hands of all the "Eddies," and most of its history books written by them. He said his object in life was to undermine, by careful, well-documented writing, the entire northern myth about the South from 1876, and thus use his scholarship to force those who taught history courses to a "higher position." His anger at Vanderbilt multiplied when Ransom fled to Kenyon. He urged Tate to blast the administration from the outside, to expose to the public "the working of the maggots." Later, he described all the years after Ransom left Vanderbilt as a "nightmare."[16]

By 1941, Owsley hated a cowardly Chancellor Carmichael as

much as he had hated Kirkland and tried to organize opposition to a new, compulsory retirement system. In his view, the administration, particularly Carmichael and his sycophantic shadow, Vice Chancellor Madison Sarratt, thought Agrarianism and hell-raising had a common identity and thus viewed the surviving Agrarians as enemies. By then, he and Davidson had no clout. He ruefully predicted that Eddie Mims would live long enough to prevent Tate from ever joining the Vanderbilt faculty. All his seething resentments against Vanderbilt came to a head in 1947, when a new chancellor, Harvie Branscomb, turned out to be even worse than his predecessors. He came with a heretical goal—to make Vanderbilt a national university, or in Owsley's view a northern one. Branscomb even wanted to downgrade southern history and refused to provide the financial commitment needed to keep the *Journal of Southern History* at Vanderbilt. Owsley had to get out. He had earlier turned down offers to come to the University of Alabama, back to his home state. In 1949 he accepted an excellent offer and left Vanderbilt with a sense of liberation.[17]

If Owsley was disillusioned with Vanderbilt, he was even more dismayed, even frightened, by national and international events. After 1936 he slowly lost all hope in Roosevelt. He bitterly resented new attacks on the South and particularly antilynching legislation. All along he had merged the twin devils of industrialism and communism, but by the late thirties he seemed most preoccupied with communists or with their labor union allies. In 1938, in a letter to an American fascist, he noted his opposition to fascist policies, to any totalitarian approach, but acknowledged the need for powerful organizations to cope with the communist virus and thus conceded that "your fascist party" may be useful. The hinterlands, the people of the South, would never accept either fascism or communism, but they might let fascists help put down those "human rats."

By World War II, Owsley knew the world was going to hell, and quickly. In 1943 he noted a visit by John Wade and dreamed that the Agrarians were reassembling, in an unconscious rallying. So much was at stake by then—"the freedom, strength and self-respect of the southern white people," even the fate of "constitutional democracy in the United States." He admitted his defection from the Democratic Party, from formerly liberal or radical economic views.

By then he proclaimed himself not even a conservative but "a reactionary." On issues of race and the "dictatorship of the proletariat," he sided with John C. Calhoun. If he had the unwanted choice between big business and big labor, he would choose big business. Earlier, the masters of capital had been robber barons, but the masters of labor were thugs, John L. Lewis a "neanderthal cannibal." By the next year, he was so angry at the "loss of constitutional principles" that, he said, if he were younger he would either flee to Australia or New Zealand or else launch a revolution. By 1955, a year before his death, and after the 1954 Supreme Court decision on integration, he remained bitter, and identified with the extreme anticommunist movement. He continued to make dire predictions about the future. The prejudices of the North would insure that the nation could not last another half century, for America had become a "mongrelized state with its contempt and suspicion of tradition and gentility." The barbarians were already poised in the Soviet Union and in China, as well as already clustered in American cities. The North, at war with the South, was balkanized by central and southern Europeans, Negroes, Puerto Ricans, and Zionists, who waxed righteous over the lynching of a Negro rapist and ignored juvenile criminals in their own midst.[18]

Mixed in with such apocalyptic foreboding were his nostalgic memories of the agrarian brethren. These memories solaced. Even as the group began to scatter in 1935, Owsley referred to a possible Thanksgiving get-together as like the old days, when we "congregated at some point and got drunk." In 1946, when it was all over, he referred to the brethren with longing, as if to another age, another planet, when they thought the world in a terrible mess, and "we had so much fun saving it, and we had a group of men almost capable of saving it — except it was so much fun to see that damn universe go to hell because it deserved it." By 1946 it had gone to hell, and no one could put it back. But he so wished the old crowd could assemble, have a few beers, and even fiddle while Russia bombed New York "and other deserving places such as Chicago, Detroit — and Nashville." Despite Ransom's defection, Owsley did not change his opinion on any fundamental agrarian question. In 1952, in response to questions from a magazine editor, he again looked back to Agrarianism, but with some changed perspectives. He stressed his desire for a balanced economy, even one with a place for a few large landowners. In the 1930s he saw industrial capitalism as a failure; in 1952 he wanted locally-owned industries for the South and by then most wanted to stress the religious content of Agrarianism and its opposition to communism. In 1955 he referred to the "old gang," the faithful few.

In April 1956, Owsley was invited to the Fugitive reunion at Vanderbilt. There he gave his final verdict on Agrarianism. Perhaps the Agrarians had lacked the right economic tools, but they had led a "revolt against materialism," and had defended, with the South as an example, the central values of Western civilization. And now they had clearly lost, as America was losing those same values, lapsing into materialism. Owsley, shortly thereafter, went to England for a year on a Fulbright grant, only to die unexpectedly. He was the first of the eight central brethren to go but, of the original twelve, both Kline and Fletcher predeceased him. [19]

Lytle shared much of Owsley's nostalgia. He rarely saw any of the agrarian brethren and missed them. In 1939 he wrote to Owsley: "We had such a grand time when all the agrarian brothers were fighting and socializing together. We are scattered, now, for good, I guess. It was a shock for me to get accustomed to acting alone. I don't suppose there has ever been so congenial a literary group, nor one which enjoyed itself so well. We ought to be grateful for that." But, at least momentarily, he believed the powers of evil had triumphed, else they might have founded a school of writing and political economy in Nashville. In 1950 he said he thought often of "our small community," back before the powers of darkness (the Vanderbilt administration) scattered it. He had been a wanderer ever since, and missed it so. In 1956, from a teaching post at the University of Florida, he wrote Owsley for the last time, noting integration efforts there. NAACP attacks on him, and his plan to send his daughter not to scalawag Vanderbilt but to Southwestern at Memphis. [20]

Davidson was the spiritual brother to Owsley and Lytle. If anything, he suffered even more the political and social changes in America. He stuck it out at Vanderbilt, as a minority, lonely, but at times courageous voice on campus, horrified at each new chancellor and at every capitulation to national values. Unlike all the other former Agrarians, he kept up the fight for the cause as he understood it. He wrote numerous, often repetitious essays, traveled anywhere to lecture, spoke out publicly on political issues, and finally, in his belated battle against integration, became the head of a political organization. Up through World War II, he somehow blended his two agrarian faces—on one side, a balanced, historically informed, eloquent defender of an agrarian program, on the other, an embattled defender of the South's racial settlement. Soon after 1945 race became his obsession, and in his last years his views of Agrarianism were almost entirely shaped by this one issue. Not that he gave all his life to a defensive stand against a new reconstruction. He remained a complex person, sweet and genial towards friends, a devoted and superb teacher of creative writing, a periodically active lyrical poet, an increasingly well-informed folklorist, a sometimes balanced and acutely perceptive essayist, a talented historian, a perceptive observer of the new country music industry in Nashville, and, each summer, a faithful New Englander during his residence in Vermont.

Until World War II, Davidson acted as if the Agrarians still had a winning program. The sharp new depression of late 1937 and early 1938 seemed, once again, to vindicate all their criticism of the old order. Davidson also hoped, despite the dispersal, to keep the agrarian circle at least loosely united. Fortunately, he did not yet realize the degree of Ransom's defection. In 1938 and 1939 he tried to remain loyal to the Agrarian-Distributist program, although he still felt that the Agrarians had been sidetracked by Agar and that they should have published their own symposium. Davidson even seemed a bit jealous of the in-group, overly resentful of outsiders. Thus, he kept making excuses, or bending his own views, to accommodate those of the original twelve brethren.

In 1939, Davidson wrote one of his most balanced and accommodating essays on Agrarianism. It was a response to historian C. Vann Woodward's review of H. C. Nixon's *Forty Acres and a Steel Mule,* and to Jonathan Daniels's *A Southerner Discovers the South.* Woodward, quite correctly, had pointed to the strong class emphasis in Nixon and used this to disassociate him from the other Agrarians. Davidson tried to give the kindest possible reading to Nixon, and to so loosen the meaning of Agrarianism as to keep him in the group. Despite the class rhetoric and too much favoritism to planning and centralized control—these all disturbed Davidson—he still believed Nixon's book was primarily factual, concerned with the detailed problems of farmers, laborers, and Negroes. Nixon still agreed that large-scale industrialization was not desirable for the South. This was enough. Nixon, like all the Agrarians, had his own private view. The movement had a core of principles but had never required a rigid dogma or orthodoxy. The group did not purge anyone, for the group did not reflect that type of solidarity. Each individual had elaborated the principles differently, and the group had never agreed on detailed programs. Davidson noted several internal differences—Nixon's class emphasis, the rejection by Young of the subsistence motifs of Lytle, the idiosyncratic elitism of Fletcher, and Owsley's exceptional enthusiasm for agricultural cooperatives. He could have added his own intense interest in regionalism. But behind the differences he saw the group as still united in opposition to large corporate enterprise, and in concern for small farmers, or what he called the democracy of the South. In brief, they were all Jeffersonians or, as he had earlier suggested, disciples of John Taylor (Lytle had published an appreciative and perceptive essay on Taylor).

Davidson even noted that the Agrarians had not shirked the problem of the Negro. He primarily referred to Warren's essay without admitting that he had tried to keep it out of *I'll Take My Stand*. After again stressing the sectional and not the class sources of most southern problems, Davidson wrote his last conciliatory statement about blacks. He stressed that, for southerners, an emphasis upon the race issue was only a way of confusing issues, making the plight of Negroes worse, and fatally postponing needed economic solutions for the rural South. To proceed on economic lines, not social, did not mean a denial of the Negro's humanity or any injustice to him, but only a continuation of the existing separate status. Davidson believed that, since emancipation, blacks had needed a special, protected status, like Native Americans, but he did not clarify exactly how such would have worked.[21]

In 1943, Davidson again tried to keep up the fiction of a continued and unified movement. In a short article in the *Saturday Review*, he tried to correct all the misinterpretations, to prove that the

Agrarians were not sentimentalists, lost in nostalgia, and out to re-store the antebellum South, but "grimly realistic," determined to tell the truth about seventy tragic years of southern history. They sought out fundamental and deep solutions, not the weak remedies of liberals or Marxists. He also refuted the popular view that the Agrarians were bookish professors, pontificating about an agriculture they did not know firsthand. Davidson cited their rural background, their familiarity with farming, the fact that most of them did know how to hitch the mules and plow a field, and that several agrarians (Lytle, Nixon, Owsley, Wade) had managed large plantations. The only common beliefs uniting the diverse group were the principles in *I'll Take My Stand*. Dozens of subsequent articles, by the twelve and other disciples, had filled out the practical implications. To know Agrarianism was to do a lot of reading, not only on political and economic issues but in history, poetry, and literary criticism, or the product of two dozen or more of the most fertile and productive minds in America. And all this writing made up "one body of thought, although all do not say the same thing." This was his desperate, even mythic effort to keep the unity that had never been there, not even in 1930.[22]

By World War II, Davidson was increasingly obsessed with racial issues, even as his long friendship with Ransom and Tate began to erode. In the early thirties the Agrarians had largely finessed the issue of race. They did not take a stand on the role or place of the Negro. They deliberately avoided the subject, save for Warren's "Briar Patch" essay, which was not likely to offend many people, North or South. Owsley first publicly engaged the issue in a controversial article. In 1933 he wrote, and tried at first unsuccessfully to find a publisher for, an article on the Scottsboro case (blacks in northern Alabama accused and convicted of rape on the basis of flimsy evidence), an article originally entitled "Crusaders: Abolition, Reconstruction, Scottsboro." The agreement with Collins allowed him to place it in the *American Review* under the title "Scottsboro, The Third Crusade; The Sequel to Abolition and Reconstruction." It amounted to a vitriolic attack on all northern intervention in southern internal affairs and, more indirectly, a defense of tough measures taken in the South to control blacks. Davidson warmly applauded the article. In more restrained terms, so did Tate. Fletcher raved about it and wrote a sharp attack on liberal and radical views of the South for the *Nation.* Davidson backed this with a letter, stressing that well-meaning and humane reformers could neither end lynching nor help the Negro. All three men now accepted a common refain—the South had to solve its own problems, particularly those involving blacks.[23]

Fortunately for the unity and reputation of the Agrarians, the Scottsboro article was exceptional. In the mid-depression years most public attention centered on economic issues. But, even in the New Deal, several Roosevelt advisors worked for racial justice, and Owsley, Davidson, and Wade, in particular, were aware of this New Deal undertone. They soon viewed Eleanor Roosevelt as the devil incarnate and worried that a left-wing group of advisors would gain ascendency in the Roosevelt administration. In 1934, in a foreboding observation, Davidson asked Wade: what about the communist intellectuals? What if Roosevelt, the American Kerenski, failed? What if the left took over? Then Wade would see his plantation divided up among his Negro tenants. Then he would have to teach nonbourgeois classics to "a class where kinky-heads and blond tresses mix in critical appraisal, and do not even nod politely—and all this for a pittance, or for nothing, while you live with your aged mother (for whom you cannot get medicine), in an apartment designated by the local committee."[24]

Davidson's worst fears seemed justified by the late thirties, with the increased effort in Congress to pass antilynching legislation. For Davidson, the Negro issue seemed to bring out his worst traits—a defensive rigidity or dogmatism. His fears went well beyond the prospect of northern intervention. He revealed a type of resentment against blacks, or at least a resentment against the solicitude shown them by writers, musicologists, and reformers. He took pains, in his writings on folklore, to deny any originality or creativity to blacks, even for their spirituals, and steadfastly refused to give any credit to Negro writers. It incensed him when southern writers focused on blacks—a modern form of sentimentality. He was hurt, even offended, when Tate in his novel, *The Fathers,* included as a character a mulatto brother of one of the white heroes. He was disappointed at Will Alexander's appointment to head the Farm Security Administration in 1937; he believed Alexander was concerned only with the problem of Negroes. Charles Sumner would have approved the appointment. It was as if the blacks were not part of the South. Eventually even Tate accused him of writing about only half the South—the white part.[25]

With World War II and national agitation for equal employment opportunities for blacks, Davidson finally aired his racial beliefs in public. To Tate he had already clarified his perspective. He approved separate but equal treatment for blacks, at least before the law, except for the suffrage. Blacks, at least in parts of the South, were too numerous and too inclined to vote as a block. In his opinion, ninety percent of blacks were ten thousand years off from any ability to govern themselves. He admitted that, if they were dispersed over the country, their condition might approach that of whites. He published these views in 1945 in the *Sewanee Review*. He admitted that the problem of blacks sprang in large part from a social disease that particularly afflicted white southerners—race prejudice. It allowed no quick or easy remedy. With his usual glee he attacked "sociologists" who wanted to legislate a remedy, just as had the ogres of reconstruction back in 1868. Such social scientists ignored southern history. Negroes came to America as slaves, stripped of a cultural heritage, forced to borrow bits and pieces of a white culture. It was not their fault. They were victims. But they suffered the continuing liability of cultural dispossession. In attitudes so deep as to be inarticulate, white southerners had all but compacted to keep blacks subordinate. By separation, and required deference, blacks were able to remain in the South, but could not enter white society. Of course, from an abstract, universalist, long view, the whites were the guilty party, backward and prejudiced. In this perspective, blacks might appear as innocent, blameless, and righteous, a sentimental view of blacks he attributed to Marxists, Negro elites, and northern reformers.

What was the answer? Davidson believed there was no early solution, at least from the black perspective. History, custom, tradition lay behind racial patterns in the South. These interacted with all aspects of southern culture, were inseparably tied to the seamless totality of a complex region which, by almost any view, might have aspects both good and bad. But such a culture never fit the abstractions of any theory, and abstract answers would not fit, or alter, it.

No legislative remedies could help speed the tortoise-like pace of change. He viewed efforts to gain a fair employment practices committee, antilynching legislation, abolition of the poll tax, federal controls over elections, and even national equal marriage laws as all part of an outside, imposed, and tyrannical attack upon the South, an attack rooted in a frightful misunderstanding of the nature of humankind and of culture. Southerners knew—if not abstractly, at least in their bones—that the Negro came as a slave, in an inferior role, and was allowed to remain only on that condition. Whites simply wanted to protect their own race, to avoid biological mingling, not to abuse blacks. Segregation was a working mode of coexistence, a condition of tolerance for blacks. In some ways it restricted whites as well as blacks. It meant continued, open defiance of the illegitimately ratified Fourteenth and Fifteenth Amendments. And the white South was not about to give up these customs and traditions. Southerners would fight. Misguided liberal reformers could only turn a peaceful racial settlement into open violence and warfare, and no one could gain from that. Those who backed legal change had a heavy responsibility, for they were forcing a new and bitter reconstruction upon an unwilling and defiant South.[26]

Davidson never backed away from this view. He had long since defined himself as a southerner. He was loyal but not always happy. In Vermont he was able, by way of contrast, to chart the terrible problems and deficiencies of the South, even as at home he tried to grasp its virtues. But one needed to have a home, be part of a tradition. This was his. And it was a complex tradition. Racial attitudes were part and parcel of white self-identity. In moments of detachment, as an intellectual, he could analyze the components of such a culture, or express his preference for alterations. He was not against change, reform, when the impulse came from within. As an intellectual he could understand, even applaud, the humane concerns of northern intellectuals. But when under siege he rallied to the cause of his country, his tradition. He wanted all southerners to do the same and was most impatient with those he identified as southern "liberals," those who became enervated because of all their distinctions and qualifications or out of abstract reasoning even joined the enemy. They then became traitors, and soon most southern academics struck him as either emasculated observers or

Donald Davidson, wife, daughter, and granddaughter at the time of his
retirement from Vanderbilt

cultural traitors. With a sense of liberation, Davidson repudiated almost all southern intellectuals and enlisted enthusiastically in the campaign for Dixiecrat Strom Thurmond in 1948.

In a sense, the expected apocalypse came with the desegregation decision of 1954. Davidson felt he had to act, to go beyond his increasingly shrill verbal assaults. Yet he was not willing to take the low road, to join the burgeoning white citizens councils, to fall into populistic anti-intellectualism or sheer demagoguery. Thus he helped form, and headed, what he wanted to be a principled defender of the old order, the Tennessee Federation for Constitutional Government. It never had much power. It was an elitist or almost academic counterpart to a largely demagogic, but briefly successful, southern counterattack from 1954 to 1960. In consequence, Davidson suffered a near complete loss of academic standing because of his active defense of segregation, despite his Calhoun-like appeal to constitutionalism and state rights. He tried to gain intellectual respectability within a new, loosely organized conservative movement, and in an article for William Buckley's *National Review* did as able a job as possible in fitting a southern defense of segregation within a broader conservative tradition.

Davidson embarrassed the Vanderbilt administration by his public stand, gained only small minority support from his faculty colleagues, and, on top of all of this, was completely ineffective. The South, from his perspective, fell once again under the sway of northern power. And not another Agrarian joined the cause, at least openly (Owsley was soon dead or he might have). By 1954, Davidson was personally closer to John Wade than to any other of his former friends. Wade, so much a part of the old order, was confused and near despair. He applauded Davidson's courage, his political role, but never had the temperament to fight back in a political way. To Wade, the unimaginable was happening. The ideal of a pure white race was falling: "Now here we are, with the entire reputable world bent, and bent with Power-at-hand, to convince us that what we took to be the 'highest virtue' is in truth the worst of vices." Typically for Wade, he could only exclaim—"Lordy me. Lordy me!"[27]

Davidson's extreme racial views, his defensive provincialism, and his ideological rigidity gradually helped erode his former friendship with Ransom and Tate. The three musketeers of 1930 went separate ways. After 1945, Ransom and Davidson scarcely spoke to each other for ten years. Tate remained friends to both, wrote to both, swapped criticism with both, but distance, divergent causes, a growing difference in beliefs, destroyed the early intimacy. The glue of friendship was largely that of shared memories. Davidson suffered most from the loss. He needed friends, encouragement, support. Without it he easily fell into self-pity, and this in turn fanned his radicalism.

Even as Davidson mourned the slackening of agrarian activity, Tate and Ransom worried about "Don." By 1936 he seemed to withdraw from the easy sociability of the group. He was always touchy, quick to make a point of principle or to reject cooperation with groups outside Nashville. In 1939, Ransom confessed, sadly, that "Don stopped growing before the rest of us did." This was unfair, for in later years Davidson wrote as much, and as well, as Ransom. But Ransom sensed the effect of ideology on Davidson and noted that Davidson, like so many southerners, was his own worst enemy. By 1942, after visiting with Davidson at Bread Loaf, Ransom wrote to Tate that Don had become hypercritical, against the government and almost everything. His negativism already threatened to destroy him.[28]

Until 1945, Davidson remained nominally a friend to Ransom. They did not break openly. But Davidson felt grieved that Ransom had deserted Agrarianism. As early as 1937 he confessed to Tate that he did not understand Ransom. He explained Ransom's defection by his lack of a historical or political outlook. Ransom never read history and thus was not prepared for New Dealism. When other answers seemed hopeless, he simply capitulated, took the best available political option. As so often, and so mysteriously, a sudden change came over John, and he took down the old flag.[29]

By 1940, Davidson felt estranged, deserted. He once lamented that his earliest mentor, Ransom, did not write him anymore and clearly did not appreciate his type of poetry. Neither did Tate. And all the fame seemed to accrue to Ransom and Tate, as almost everyone ignored Davidson. Yet, when Ransom made the effort to see Davidson at Bread Loaf in 1940 and again in 1942, these suspicions quickly evaporated, for John was, as usual, generous and friendly.

Then came the big blows. First it was Tate. He had moved to Princeton in 1939, then to the position of poetry consultant to the Library of Congress in 1943, and finally in 1944 accepted the editorship of the nearby *Sewanee Review.* This brought him, for a brief period of just over a year, back into the Nashville orbit. But Tate, in an editorial in the *Review,* had taken a much more generous view towards blacks (albeit still a segregationist view) than Davidson, and in particular had defended equality with separation as a protection for blacks. Davidson reprimanded him, insisting that the welfare of blacks was a secondary concern, that segregation was a protective device for whites, who quite openly and justifiedly denied to them full citizenship or equal protection of the law. This marked a break in sentiment, one soon to deepen, between Davidson and the person he always considered his closest friend. Tate never allowed an open break. He bent over backward to accommodate Don, to concede all he could to his views. But the bonds slowly weakened.

Much worse was Ransom's treason. He not only used a 1945 article to repudiate his earlier Agrarianism, but he sent a copy to Davidson. This seemed salt on a wound. To Davidson, Ransom had completely distorted Agrarianism, accepting all the critics' charges that it was a nostalgia trip. He now made Mencken seem like a prophet. The Ransom of the North now talked out the opposite side of his mouth from the Ransom of the South. Even his refined essays on esthetics were in conflict with his earlier, basic principles. He vowed never to write John again, not even to correct all the errors in his article. In his hurt, silence seemed the best response. Davidson thus cut the ties and was soon absorbed in doing, and doing brilliantly, what he believed Ransom never appreciated—history. He wrote an eloquent two-volume history of the Tennessee River, the second volume of which gained him a deserved Pulitzer Prize. He remained bitter. He almost rejoiced when he heard that Ransom was in trouble at Kenyon, yet saw even that as a backhanded way for northerners to get back at the Agrarians.[30]

In 1955, when the English department at Vanderbilt wanted to invite Ransom back as a visitor, Davidson protested. Ransom had left of his own free will and then changed sides morally and ideologically. He had repudiated Agrarianism and was now deeply committed to the "other side." Davidson was more right than he knew.

In 1955, Ransom had written to Warren about the desegregation decision. He noted how divided his sentiments were but on balance agreed with Warren that their sympathies should be strong and decisive for desegregation. Davidson was fearful of what would happen if Ransom visited Vanderbilt. He asked: "If he comes down talking socialism, racial amalgamation, and so forth . . . what do you think would happen?" If he came and took a "leftist-liberal" position, Davidson would have to take a public stand against him, creating a "hot situation." He suggested the forthcoming Fugitive reunion as a substitute. But, after ten years, Ransom wrote a cordial letter about the distribution of royalties from a new and well-selling edition of I'll Take My Stand (3,402 copies by 1963), and Davidson, as always, responded in kind. He was all but incapable of rudeness on a one-to-one basis. Ransom did not come to teach until the fall of 1961, after retiring at Kenyon, but by the Fugitive reunion of 1956 he and Davidson talked as if nothing had divided them. They even shared an office in 1961. But, of course, such a personal reconciliation did nothing to bridge the wide gulf that separated their beliefs and values. They simply avoided sensitive political issues.[31]

Ransom's last years were full of honors, but made less fulfilling by poor health and a clear decline in mental vigor. Ironically, at a time when he wrote no poems, or merely fooled around with old ones, he received the Bollinger Prize for his selected poems (1945 edition), the National Book Award for his selected poems (1963), and was honored by membership in the National Institute of Arts and Letters (1947) and the American Academy of Arts and Letters (1966). Testimonials, or festschrifts, marked his seventy-fifth and eightieth birthdays. In the last years, bouts of dizziness made walking almost impossible and ended his writing. He came to the University of Dallas in 1968 to attend a southern literary festival and was able to have a reunion with Tate, the principal speaker. In 1973, in his last public appearance, he was able to introduce Robert Penn Warren for a lecture at Kenyon. He died on 3 July 1974, at the advanced age of 86, or fifty-four years after publication of the first Fugitive.

The friendship of Tate and Davidson survived all the strains. It took forbearance on both sides, particularly Tate's. Both reviewed each other's books, usually with enthusiastic praise, although Tate

Robert Penn Warren as introduced by John Crowe Ransom at Kenyon in
1973, their last meeting and Ransom's last public appearance (Photo by
Carswell Berlin)

continued to carp at Davidson's lyrical, ideologically tinged poems (*The Long Street* in 1961 and *Poems, 1922–61,* in 1966). The postwar years remained turbulent ones for Tate. He and Caroline could not live together in harmony, yet could not live apart. Tension and a divorce at the end of the war led to a reunion, remarriage, and desperate efforts to preserve the marriage. In the midst of this effort, both moved toward conversion to Catholicism. Although both Ransom and Davidson had long expected this, and gave their blessings, the move also touched deep loyalties and prejudices. To an extent, it further separated Tate from the brethren, since he, as so many converts, professed complete loyalty to the truths taught by the Church. Davidson, somewhat surprisingly, said he had thought of joining the Church himself. Old loyalties held him back, as did his lingering intellectual skepticism and his distrust for preachers. He said he respected Roman Catholicism and the Primitive Baptists, but "Lord deliver me from the Methodists, the Baptists in general, from most of the Episcopal lot, the Presbyterians, and the rest." By the reunion of 1956, the two seemed as close, as affectionate, as back in the twenties.[32]

But Tate had to tolerate a great deal, for by then Davidson was off on his political crusade for segregation. Before this, he had echoed the outlook of Joseph McCarthy, had supported a loyalty oath for Tennessee (against most of his faculty colleagues), and even argued that communists (always unidentified) controlled Phi Beta Kappa. In 1962, after receiving endless diatribes from Davidson on the racial situation, Tate clarified his own position. He pointed out that no one could prevent desegregation, ridiculed southern doctrines of nullification or interposition (no one had believed in these since 1832), and noted that secession was not an available choice in 1962, as it had been in 1861. More directly preaching to Davidson, he lamented Confederate flag-waving and invocation of state rights only on race issues. This gave the case away. He and Ransom had talked recently. Both had strong attachments to the Old South. Both confessed that they would probably feel uncomfortable in an integrated South. "I would not know how to conduct myself." He even acknowledged that, in his opinion, the Supreme Court blundered. This was all he would concede. By then, even the authority of his Church supported compliance, which he recommended for the South. It had no alternative, and no good could come from violent resistance. The South should take over the process of desegregation and do it "with order and dignity." Tate confessed that he was in favor of Negro rights, but felt the courts should have begun with Negro voting rights, not school integration. The Negro had to get the vote, let the chips fall where they may. Maybe the blacks, where in a majority, would impose a new segregation and the whites would have to move. So be it.

A month later, Tate further chided Davidson. He was amazed that the southern way of life became critical only when race relations were upset. "If there isn't more to the southern way of life than this, it is not worth fighting for." After all, Mississippians had rejected Agrarianism, invited industrialists to come down, and now affirmed the southern way by rioting. Tate soon disagreed with Davidson on another, unrelated issue. Davidson wanted censorship to prevent the publication of such novels as *Lady Chatterly's Lover*. Tate, as in the past, fought for freedom of the press. The conflicting racial views, as Davidson knew, reflected a dramatic shift from Tate's position back in the twenties and thirties. He, almost as much as Ransom, had accommodated change. Davidson never would.[33]

Of the three, Davidson died first but, unlike Ransom, he was active and alert almost to the end. Except on the political side, he had a very productive old age. His interests, if anything, widened. Nothing ever gave him more satisfaction than music. In 1952, in a high point of his life, he wrote a folk opera, *Singin' Billy*, which Charles Faulkner Bryan, a Peabody composer, set to music. The performance at Vanderbilt was a tremendous success and would be followed by a few performances elsewhere in the South. Davidson completed two final volumes of essays, rejoiced in a 1962 paperbound version of *I'll Take My Stand* (the bestseller of all the editions), and retired from Vanderbilt in 1964, but continued summer teaching at Bread Loaf. In the same year John Wade died. By then, he was the closest soul mate to Davidson, and Marshallville almost a second or third home. Davidson wrote a moving introduction in 1966 to a volume of Wade's essays, the last book he edited. His interest had turned almost completely to folk music, religion, and the past. His last essay, "The Center That Holds: Southern Literature and the Old Time Religion," was the text of a speech delivered in Charleston, South

Carolina. He blessed the older form of evangelical religion in the South, arguing for the deeply rooted religious consciousness of southerners, which anchored all the myths and stories and even helped account for the southern literary renaissance. Without this, and the southern sense of history, the blessings of family and community, that literature would soon wither and die.[34]

But who was around to keep the faith? He confessed that, as a form of last punishment, he read all the revisionist literature about the South, with C. Vann Woodward leading the devilish pack. Davidson felt out of phase, an anachronism. In his last two years he poured all of his efforts into a novel. To Tate, he apologized for the more torrid scenes or dialogues. In fact, it was almost Victorian in its language. Entitled *The Big Ballad Jamboree,* with a plot never quite satisfactorily resolved, it set up a tension between modern country music, represented by a young male singer, and the older, authentic folk music, worshiped with almost religious intensity by a young woman scholar. Heavily nuanced, full of human weaknesses on both sides, and with a suppressed romantic angle, it had publication possibilities. In its depiction of inspired hillbilly concerts it remains the most perceptive and sympathetic account of the new forms of country music then booming in Nashville. Davidson died on 25 April 1968.[35]

The younger Tate, despite his chain-smoking and his turbulent life, outlived both Davidson and Ransom. After editing the *Sewanee Review* in 1944–45, dramatically increasing its prestige and circulation, he worked as a literary editor for Henry Holt, became a lecturer at New York University, a visitor at the University of Chicago, before finally gaining a permanent professorship at the University of Minnesota in 1951. He published several volumes of essays, constantly recasting and reusing past performances, and likewise kept issuing selections of his poems, always with a few new ones. In 1955, and in defiance of his church, he and Caroline finally separated for good. After a divorce in 1959, he married Isabella Gardner, only to divorce her in 1966. A third marriage, to Helen Heinz, endured, and brought him domestic peace and a new family—three sons, though one, a twin, died as a child. In 1967, before Davidson died, Tate finally gained that long-deferred appointment at Vanderbilt—he taught in the spring semester. After retiring in 1968 from

Allen Tate as Visiting Professor of English at Vanderbilt, 1967 (Photo by Gerald Holly)

Minnesota, he moved back to Sewanee, where he taught until 1975, and then in 1976 moved to Nashville. By then ill with emphysema, he died on 9 February 1979. In his last years he received numerous honors, although not quite as many as Ransom. He, like Ransom, became a member of both the American Academy of Arts and Letters and the American Academy of Arts and Sciences, and deservedly ranks as one of the ablest critics in American literary history.

Three agrarians survived Tate. Only Lytle still upheld the old cause. Lyle Lanier moved on to become provost and executive vice-president of the University of Illinois. Robert Penn Warren remained at LSU until 1942, then moved to the University of Minnesota, and on to Yale University in 1950, where he served as professor in the School of Drama until retirement. He finally divorced the troubled Cinina in 1950 and remarried, happily, at long last gaining the security of home and children. Eventually, Warren bought a three-acre homestead in Connecticut and as a gardener kept a sentimental tie to his agrarian past. Because of his achievement as both novelist and poet, in addition to some perceptive criticism, he became the most famous of the ex-Agrarians and America's first poet laureate. Agrarianism was no longer a significant component of his identity. More vital to him had been his lifelong friendship with both Tate and Ransom.

Lytle kept his ties to Tennessee, even during his tenure at the University of Florida from 1948 to 1961. He then returned to Sewanee, to teach at the University of the South and to edit the *Sewanee Review* from 1961 to 1972. He gained most fame as a novelist. In retirement he continues to live in Monteagle, where the Agrarians of old so often gathered. In 1980 the three survivors—Lanier, Lytle, Warren—returned to Vanderbilt for a final Agrarian reunion and to participate in a conference on Agrarianism fifty years after publication of *I'll Take My Stand*. Only Lytle, echoing the old themes, seemed an unreconstructed believer. Through subsequent years, in letters, in pungent essays, in interviews, he has kept up the fight. Finally, in a sense, Agrarianism had shrunk to the early "kid" of the group, to the ever faithful Andrew.

Robert Penn Warren, Andrew Lytle, Lyle Lanier, and Cleanth Brooks at
the Agrarian Reunion, Vanderbilt, 1980 (Photo by Jeff Carr)

Epilogue

I have told my story. Some reflections are in order. In one sense, I have been hard on the Southern Agrarians. I have offered judgments that they would have resented, or made careful distinctions that they could not have made at the time. I have noted inconsistencies or superficialities in their thought. Thus, my effort has been erosive, most clearly in denying to them at any time the collective unity they wanted or claimed. They tried to nourish commonalities, points of agreement. I have searched for points of tension and tried to clarify even the subtle differences that underlay a common vocabulary. In fact, one might protest that I have practically dissolved any common core of meaning for the label "Southern Agrarian." Not quite, as I will argue later.

On the other hand, as much or more than any previous scholar, I have tried to take the beliefs and goals of the Agrarians quite seriously. Too often, the literary fame of key Agrarians, or their very eloquence, has diverted attention from their political and economic analysis or their proposed programs. The easiest put-down of all is to dismiss their varied, and at times ambivalent, critique of American society as metaphorical or symbolic, and thus as something quite other than what it seemed on the surface. After all, one argument goes, they were artists, not economists or acute social critics.

I deplore such a tactic for evading the content of their criticism. It is as unfair as it is ahistorical.

It is because I take their beliefs and preferences seriously that I have subjected them to close analysis. The erosive aspects of my story thus complement an underlying sympathy for the main actors. Both in producing *I'll Take My Stand,* and in their later, more programmatic policy advocacy, all the Agrarians took on the role of social critics. Southern Agrarianism identifies not a literary genre but a loosely focused point of view about the requirements of a humane and fulfilling social order. Their moral and prophetic role united them in purpose with other critics who made a very different diagnosis of American ills or who preached very different remedies. For example, *I'll Take My Stand* bears comparison with what are arguably the two most influential contemporary American works of social criticism, Reinhold Niebuhr's *Moral Man and Immoral Society* and John Dewey's *Liberalism and Social Action.* Because of its multiple authors, *I'll Take My Stand* could not be as coherent, as well focused as these two books. But with only two or three exceptions, its essays were both clearer and more eloquent, although less fashionable, than those written by Niebuhr and Dewey, both of whom advocated collectivist rather than proprietary goals.

Another, related way to characterize the Agrarians is as reformers. But the label is so general, so loose, that it does not discriminate. In some sense, almost everyone wants certain changes, wants to reform this or that institution. The Agrarians could never match the breadth and verve of their critique of modern America with persuasive solutions. That was equally true of Niebuhr and Dewey, as it is of most critics. But after 1933 the Agrarians tried to develop a practical reform agenda, one necessarily fitted to the realities and confusions of a depression. As it turned out, this was the last brief period in twentieth-century America when strategies for the restoration of property, for efforts to decentralize production, to move back toward subsistence agriculture, or even seriously to propose a homestead program for landless rural and urban workers, had any widespread appeal. The occasion passed so quickly that it is no wonder that subsequent historians of the Agrarians, when at all sympathetic, have felt the need to dismiss or apologize for their restorationist program or else to read into it a largely metaphorical content. In fact, their proposals were no more quickly dated than most other rejected depression options, from technocracy to communism. The mild regulatory-welfare state that grew apace during, and then survived, the depression won such a complete policy victory in America as to make all more extreme proposals of the thirties, whether classed as radical or reactionary, seem in retrospect naive or utopian or even foolish. But such criticism had enduring value as a challenge to American institutions. Undoubtedly, the prophet Micah seemed to be a naive, unrealistic reactionary to his seventh-century B.C.E. Judean audience.

I have emphasized the distinction between the Agrarianism of *I'll Take My Stand* and that of the more programmatic movement launched in 1933. The overlap is considerable but far from complete. Most of the 1930 essays, some written as much as three years earlier, reflected a broad cultural critique at a very general, even philosophical level. Of course, Owsley, Warren, and Nixon offered a more concrete, empirical, or programmatic perspective, but they did not set the tone for the volume. Ransom, Fletcher, Davidson, Tate, Lanier, and Lytle did. Wade's biographical sketch also seemed to back up the broad, cultural critique of the six dominant essays, which were most consistent with Ransom's opening manifesto. These six essays, despite significant differences in outlook, all joined in condemning large firms, centralized management, alienated and hurried work, an unrelenting commitment to technical progress, an abstract, manipulative, scientific approach to nature, and the dominance of consumptive values. They posed against this the value of localized or household production, as epitomized in agriculture; of leisurely, artful, undriven, self-directed work; of a direct mythic and inherently religious understanding of nature; and of friendship and the arts of simple living.

These common and widely appealing values could not conceal some deep tensions. Ransom and Fletcher, at times even Tate, seemed to endorse an hierarchical, aristocratic, and elitist as well as established and settled social order, one made up of numerous classes but dominated by a classically educated gentry of an older English or European type. Davidson, Lytle, Owsley, and others idealized a much more classless, equalitarian society but, ironically, had much deeper commitments to Negro subordination than did a Ransom, a Tate, or at times a Fletcher. This cleavage was reflected in their diverse images of the South, past and present. In a loose way, all recognized that the South, in part because of its Civil War defeat and subsequent economic exploitation by the North, had retained much of its simpler past, including the continued economic dominance of agriculture, decentralized forms of household production, orthodox Christianity, and several nonconsumptive, nonprogressive values. It was, in this sense, not only not yet modern but still antimodern. But the "European," almost feudal Old South of a Fletcher was far from the yeoman, equalitarian, Jeffersonian South of Lytle, Owsley and Nixon.

The depression quickly dissolved most of the elitist motifs. Fletcher not only flip-flopped ideologically but eventually resigned from the group. Ransom dropped his religious-cultural themes and tried to be a good economist. Tate converted to distributism. Thus, in their post-1933 essays the remaining eight Agrarians reflected almost none of the earlier hierarchical, organic, and aristocratic themes. Just the opposite. With Owsley now a dominant voice, and Davidson by far the most prolific essayist, they celebrated a simpler yeoman society. Of course, the generalized critique of northern industrialism remained, but now this economic system was clearly the only one that was elitist, as well as exploitative and imperialistic. All the Agrarians joined in an almost populist indictment of money and privilege and joined in efforts to decentralize production, to restore productive property to as many people as possible, and to nationalize or closely regulate all remaining large firms.

Logically, the Agrarians should have embraced a single tax on land. Instead, they would have nothing to do with this traditional and strongest land reform weapon, advocated by almost all true agrarians. Such a socialization of land, as a means of guaranteeing wider access to its productive powers, ran into a reluctance that revealed the deepest snag in the programmatic Agrarian movement—a deeply rooted fear of the federal government. This issue created deep ambivalences even in individuals such as Owsley, who wanted extensive new federal economic programs, who joined Nixon in backing rural cooperatives but joined Davidson in his growing horror of federal social legislation. Behind these fears was the issue of race, an explosive issue which by itself doomed the united agrarian cause after 1937. Racial concerns also probably doomed any continued cooperation with the northern distributists and eventually splintered the Agrarians into two groups—the racial moderates or liberals (Nixon, Ransom, Tate, Warren, and Lanier) versus the die-hard defenders of segregation (Davidson, Owsley, Lytle, and Wade).

The strains and tensions never eroded the one common preference that united all the Agrarians—support for the proprietary ideal. Despite all their differences, this is the one common element that continues to give a common meaning to Southern Agrarianism. And this ideal, more than any other, accounts for the broad and continued appeal of their essays. In a sense, the Southern Agrarians led the last significant American campaign in behalf of property and the humane concerns so well expressed in the ancient right to property. One can even argue that the Agrarians were the last original group of critics in America, with anything close to a national audience, who took property and property rights seriously. An alternative way of expressing this point is that they fought the last significant, rearguard, and losing battle against either socialist or corporate forms of collectivism—against large accumulations of capital, narrowly centralized and bureaucratic management, and wage dependent, non-owning workers.

They were not original in this stand, just a bit anachronistic. For, to an extent they could not realize in the mid-thirties, the long, deeply-rooted American resistance to collectivism—to large corporations, to factory production, to economic interdependence, to employment rather than self-employment—was all but over, hopelessly defeated. The proprietary idea—that each head of a household could aspire to individual ownership of, and control over, productive property—died hard in America. In one sense, it is not yet dead. Wage and salaried workers, in government or the many private governments called corporations, still reveal in opinion polls a strong, usually frustrated desire to be free and self-sufficient, to own a small business, to be entrepreneurs, and thus not directly dependent on anyone else for their livelihood. After all, the promise of early America was just such an independent status, at least for white males, and the most crucial early American meaning for the word *liberty* entailed such independence, not the much less critical right of free expression in speech, press, or religion.

The depth of this American commitment to proprietorship helps explain the long resistance of native-born Americans to large business enterprise, to the discipline of factories and mass production, and to employee status. Native-born American workers long tried to maintain what was all too often a fiction—the temporary nature of their wage work—and thus developed little class consciousness, resisted class politics, and were often even reluctant to join labor unions. The builders of large corporate empires—the captains of industry—long seemed dangerous or un-American and faced enormous popular resentment. Only in the twenties, as the Agrarians began writing essays, did corporate America finally gain a degree of respectability and acceptance. It was this assimilation and acceptance of large collective enterprise, at times in the twenties even its celebration, that so dismayed the early Southern Agrarians. They sensed a major transposition of values. What they viewed, from Alexander Hamilton onward, as a conspiratorial subversion of American values by relatively few capitalists, had become in their day an awful system accepted by a majority of Americans. This shift in values lay behind the agrarian indictment of what they called industrialism, which referred both to a mode of economic organization and the cultural values that supported it. Such values now seemed ascendant in the society at large but not yet so in backwater areas such as the South, where the old proprietary values still dominated, even when material conditions were subverting them on all sides. In the late twenties and then, in particular, during the depression thirties, when the now dominant values seemed most tarnished and suspect, it did not seem foolish or hopelessly unrealistic to launch a counterattack.

It was in this sense that the Agrarians wrote as self-conscious cultural outsiders or aliens. They saw themselves as at cross-purposes with most intellectuals of their day. This accounts for many of their original insights. Their South remained, in several senses, a conquered province. As young southern intellectuals, they had the strongest possible motive—their identity was at stake—to find redemptive values somewhere in their southern heritage, and to find all the darkness and evil they could among northerners who had caused southern poverty and then gloated over the ignorance and backwardness of southerners. As John Shelton Reed has argued, the

Agrarians reflected a type of aggressive southern nationalism that bears comparison to that exhibited by defeated or conquered peoples of Europe. Such a regional self-consciousness, and such a sense of alienation, decisively separated them from most northern social critics, who also charted the same evils in the American economic system. The Agrarians, in their wholehearted rejection of what they eventually called finance capitalism, joined other radical critics, including Marxists, but almost all other critics believed a return to a proprietary society, to decentralized production, risked too great a sacrifice of efficiency and too large a drop in consumption. The Agrarians, almost alone, struggled unsuccessfully, in time with waning hopes, to move back as far as possible toward property and free enterprise. To them, such a backward move promised a more humane social order than one based on public interest regulation or welfare transfers. It meant restored freedom and independence in place of government paternalism.

But reality soon defeated them. They could never hope to reverse, in any major way, the collectivism already well entrenched in the North and even in southern cities. Thus, when proposing more proximate or immediate reforms, they almost all ended up supporting, for the North and even for industrial areas of the South, stiffer economic regulation, marginal nationalization, antimonopoly legislation, and more welfare. The Distributists joined them in this. But such "reforms" to the system betrayed their original, more radical rejection of an industrial system, as Ransom conceded. And the expanded government role, the federal paternalism, implicit in such economic regulation threatened the regional autonomy, the cultural distinctiveness, of a South that Davidson and Owsley so cherished. As the economy finally took off in World War II, the remaining leeway for decentralist programs shrank to near zero, and southern political leaders, with increasing fervor, eagerly joined the rest of the country in courting corporate enterprise.

Left stranded, almost helpless, were the Agrarians and thus also the older American dreams of freedom and independence. The practical alternatives were meager. One remained beguiling to many intellectuals—a fully politicized economy, with government ownership of all productive tools. But, as the Agrarians had perceived from the beginning, this classical socialist program promised less, not more, freedom; more, not less, servility. They maintained their original insight—the devil is collectivism, whether under the auspices of finance capitalism, state socialism, or communism. Finance capitalism can, indeed, offer wondrous substitutes for freedom, for ownership and a sense of involvement, for the intrinsic fulfillment of self-directed or artful work—a consumptive cornucopia. Most Americans, insofar as they had a choice, bought this payoff. By 1937, Ransom bought it, not happily, but as the only real option available. National socialism offered its substitute for proprietorship—an artifically cultivated pride in the nation and its achievements. The cost, in internal repression and external aggression, seemed high indeed. Marxist dreams of an interim socialist society, of an economic system owned and managed by workers, seemed, on the surface, an economically progressive way of gaining the involvement and self-actualization of individual ownership without sacrificing economies of scale. But the Agrarians believed the promise a mirage and viewed communism as certain to lead only to another form of state socialism, with totalitarian repression, expansionist dreams, and the inefficiencies of central planning. It is not that cooperation in itself was wrong, but that genuine, fulfilling cooperation had to be completely voluntary and local, resting upon the autonomy secured by protected individual ownership.

The equating of finance capitalism with communism distinguished the Agrarians from most American intellectuals. So did their implicit and, belatedly, quite explicit emphasis upon property. In its sources in Western moral theory, and in early conceptions of natural rights, the right to property had a positive meaning. It denoted the right of every person to share equally in what humans did not create by labor but received as a gift from a creator god. God's farm is for everyone, and a right of access to, and of productive use of, one's share of that farm is a precondition of livelihood and happiness. It is a moral or natural right; denial of access is a moral wrong. In the agrarian tradition, beginning with the Roman Gracchi, but first promoted aggressively in England by Thomas Spence at the time of the American Revolution, the right of access to nature, or what agrarians meant by property, was the primary human right and the one most difficult to protect. When a part of nature is vested exclusively in individuals through state-granted title, or when nature can be bought and sold like a labor-produced commodity, a few powerful individuals may gain an undue proportion. Such monopolies exclude others from their rightful share and raise rents to exorbitant levels. Thus, the right to property is the key to independence and the only reliable protection against servility. This argument was cherished by the Distributists and accepted by most of the Southern Agrarians, who became the most able exponents in America of a restoration of property since Henry George. In this emphasis, they revived briefly a form of radicalism quite different in its implications from almost all forms of socialism.

It was the seeming impracticality, even the near inconceivability, of their goals that seemed to doom the Agrarians to early irrelevance. Every trend in American life would soon be away from individual ownership and free enterprise, and away from distinctive local institutions. The trend lines all led toward more centralized government, larger firms, less ownership, and less local diversity. Property, in the sense of individual ownership of and managerial control over land and tools, steadily disappeared in America, replaced by immense pools of corporate capital, legal claims to a share of profit in place of ownership, hired managers in place of owner-managers, and non-owning workers in place of earlier proprietors. Neither property, in the traditional moral sense, nor work, in the sense of artistry and intrinsic goals, survived the change. In this context, what could be more radical, or dangerous, even for the South, than the restoration pushed by Southern Agrarians?

And it is in the perspective of the South that agrarian goals now seem most ironic. Although the South remains more rural than other sections, it is not thereby more agricultural. In only a few enclaves of rich soil are agricultural industries still dominant. And even here the family-owned farm seems threatened. Given the range of federal controls, the specialization, the high capital costs, the intense competitive pressures, the limits on entrepreneurial freedom posed by creditors or marketing organizations, and even southern farms now seem fully a part of an "industrial" system, or at least captive to all the values of such a system. And beyond agriculture, the South has embraced manufacturing and large firms. It eventually became the center of American manufacturing, particularly of a more labor-intensive type, and now suffers from the relative de-

cline of manufacturing in a largely service-oriented economy. Mos
critical, at least from the agrarian perspective, it welcomed anc
even subsidized collective production in its worst forms—the ugli
est factories, the lowest wages, the least protected workers, the mos
lenient state regulations, the least environmental protection. Today
southern states compete for more of the same.

These facts do not prove the Agrarians right or wrong, if it is
even correct to use such terms for values or preferences. But, in fact
these changes in the South soon made agrarian remedies seem quaint
What the Agrarians had to acknowledge were the multiple prob
lems that had long plagued southern agriculture. They realized that
an impoverished agriculture could not be the basis of a good life
As it was, southerners usually made a rational choice to give up
agriculture for wage work. They had to live. They often had children to feed, clothe, and educate, and they had their own consumptive desires, quite legitimate ones even before the artificial fanning
of modern advertising. The hard realities of a proprietary society,
one in which up to fifty percent of southern individual entrepreneurs were tenants or sharecroppers, one in which incomes barely
met subsistence needs, and one which rested upon a vicious racial
system, did little to recommend it to anyone. What does it cost to
be on one's own, to be independent, to be free? Too much for millions of Americans, farmers or shop owners, who often with deep
regrets, often with a sense of lost status, nonetheless gave up a proprietary role in order to gain an income, more consumption, and
opportunities for a family.

Unholy bargain or not, it was one in which most southerners
had little choice. And like colonial people abroad, they had to bargain at a disadvantage. Southern agriculture, when the soil and climate allowed it to remain competitive, could survive only when it
became capital intensive. Thus, it could soon provide work for no
more than five percent of the southern work force. What could all
the rest do? Since the thirties, the southern population has almost
doubled, making even more unrealistic any return to small productive units. Thus, in the southern economy, jobs became, and still
are, all-important. Southern politicians, favored by the endurance
of a New Deal coalition, were able to bid effectively, and on the
best available terms, for government and corporate investment. They

gained much of the desired employment and thus, ironically, succumbed to the one evil the Agrarians most wanted to resist. But, of course, the jobs have never been quite enough and accordingly the South has suffered more than its share of unemployment or underemployment. In such a context, even the Agrarians might admit that employment is better than proud but hungry idleness.

Since the thirties, and for the first time since the Civil War, the former Confederate states have slowly narrowed the gap in income that for so long distinguished them from the North. From less than 50 percent of national averages in 1930, this South has risen to over 80 percent today. For white southerners, incomes may match national averages. In these terms the South is more prosperous than in over a century. These economic gains have been matched, or almost matched, by improved education and other government services, narrowing the statistical lag of the South in almost every index of human achievement.

Thus, the acclaimed success of the modern sunbelt South mocks both the critique and the goals of the Southern Agrarians. But what options did the South have? Ransom, who always insisted upon the close ties between economic organization and the total culture, decided in 1937 to go along with a reformed industrialism. New regulations had corrected some of the worst abuses of corporate collectivism, at least in the North. Of course, its alienating potential remained, but that was the cost Americans had to pay for prosperity. From his perspective, the only realistic political challenge was to perfect the regulations and welfare measures needed to make such private collectivism as humane as possible. In a sense, he did sell out to the enemy as Davidson always alleged and, in a sense, so did almost all other southerners who still nourished proprietary beliefs and values but nonetheless went along with the changes.

If a return to property is now inconceivable, then the present burden of public policy is to find the "best" possible form of collectivism. This task implicates almost all the most crucial domestic policy choices facing modern states. The big question is what "best" could mean, beyond vague utilitarian truisms, such as the most happiness or fulfillment for the most people, or even more vague references to the public interest. The Agrarians have no answers for such contemporary questions. They wanted to avoid collectivism in the South, or even reverse that already developing. For this reason they offer remarkably few guidelines to present policymakers.

They do force all southerners, as well as Americans as a whole, to look closely, and critically, at present institutions. They remind us of what people lost in the transition from a proprietary to a collective economy, even as they provoke moral doubts about the consumptive returns that most, but not all people, gained. In so far as we have accepted the bargain, tacitly consented to the new order, they at least force self-examination and create a sense of guilt. Only the most insensitive and shallow person can listen, really listen, to the Agrarians without a poignant sense of loss. This is true even for those who know about all the dark corners in the proprietary past.

Notes

I. The Fugitive Prelude

1. See the letters of John Crowe Ransom, 1911–20, in *Selected Letters of John Crowe Ransom,* ed. Thomas Daniel Young and George Core (Baton Route: Louisiana State Univ. Press, 1985), 32–106.

2. Chronology of Donald Davidson in *The Literary Correspondence of Donald Davidson and Allen Tate,* ed. John Tyree Fain and Thomas Daniel Young (Athens: University of Georgia Press, 1974), 419–23; see also Davidson's letters to family members during WWI, in Box 1 (outgoing correspondence), Davidson Papers, Special Collections, Heard Library, Vanderbilt University (henceforth cited as SC).

3. Louise Cowan, *The Fugitive Group: A Literary History* (Baton Rouge: Louisiana State Univ. Press, 1959), 3–42; Louis D. Rubin, Jr., *The Wary Fugitives: Four Poets and the South* (Baton Rouge: Louisiana State Univ. Press, 1978), 2–15; Thomas Daniel Young, *Gentleman in a Dustcoat: A Biography of John Crowe Ransom* (Baton Rouge: Louisiana State Univ. Press, 1976), 37–40, 80–84, 90–93.

4. Rubin, *Wary Fugitives,* 13–14; Cowan, *Fugitive Group,* 5, 17–20; Rob Roy Purdy, ed., *Fugitives' Reunion: Conversations at Vanderbilt, May 3–5, 1956* (Nashville: Vanderbilt Univ. Press, 1959), 32, 90–91, 123–28.

5. Young, *Gentleman,* 90–93.

6. Cowan, *Fugitive Group,* 20–22, 26–28; Rubin, *Wary Fugitives,* 15–21; John Crowe Ransom, *Poems About God* (New York: Holt, 1919).

7. Cowan, *Fugitive Group,* 24–26, 28–30; Rubin, *Wary Fugitives,* 15, 21; Michael O'Brien, *The Idea of the American South, 1920–1941* (Baltimore: Johns Hopkins Univ. Press, 1979), 119–20, 185.

8. Cowan, *Fugitive Group,* 30–35.

9. Allen Tate, *Memoirs and Opinions, 1928–1974* (Chicago: Swallow Press, 1975), 3–23; Cowan, *Fugitive Group,* 30–35; Daniel Joseph Singal, *The War Within: From Victorian to Modernist Thought in the South, 1919–1945* (Chapel Hill: Univ. of North Carolina Press, 1982), 232–34; O'Brien, *American South,* 136–39; Tate, *The Fathers and other Fiction* (Baton Rouge: Louisiana State Univ. Press, 1938, 1977).

10. Cowan, *Fugitive Group,* 43–48; Rubin, *Wary Fugitives,* 2–3; *Fugitive* 1 (April 1922): 1; (Oct. 1922): 66; (Dec. 1922): 98–100.

11. Cowan, *Fugitive Group,* 55–59, 77–79.

12. Rubin, *Wary Fugitives,* 23–29; *Fugitive,* 1 (April 1922): passim; *Jade* 3 (13 April 1922); Vanderbilt University *Hustler,* 20 April 1922; Cowan, *Fugitive Group,* 53–55; Purdy, *Fugitives' Reunion,* 118; Tate, *Memoirs and Opinions,* 34.

13. Cowan, *Fugitive Group,* 105–106; *Fugitive* 2 (April–May 1923): 34.

14. See Minutes of Fugitive Meeting, in Fugitive-Agrarian Collection, Box 1, SC.

15. Cowan, *Fugitive Group,* 106–108; Singal, *War Within,* 340–42; O'Brien, *American South,* 185–87; Young, *Gentleman,* 126–27.

16. Cowan, *Fugitive Group,* 118–27, 149; Rubin, *Wary Fugitives,* 47, 82–85, 147–48; Young, *Gentleman,* 137–45, 150–57, 164. Ransom to Tate, 30 July and 17 Dec. 1923, in John Crowe Ransom Papers (copies of letters from Ransom to Tate in the Firestone Library of Princeton University, collected by Thomas Daniel Young), SC; Tate, *Memoirs and Opinions,* 39–45.

17. "Minutes of Fugitive Meeting held 5 November 1924," in Fugitive-Agrarian Collection, Box 1, SC.

18. Cowan, *Fugitive Group,* 117–22, 139–40, 155–57, 190, 216–21.

19. Davidson to Tate, 29 July 1926, 23 Feb. 1927; Tate to Davidson, 19 Jan. 1927, 20 Jan. 1927, 1 March 1927, 7 March 1927, in *Correspondence of Davidson and Tate,* pp. 174–95; Ransom to Tate, [Fall] 1927, Ransom Papers (Young collection).

20. Tate to Davidson, 20 June 1922, 28 June 1922, 29 June 1923, 8 Dec. 1924, in Davidson Papers, Box 10.

21. Davidson to father, 8 Feb. 1919, Davidson Papers, Box 1.

22. Tate to Davidson, 20 Feb. 1927, Davidson Papers, Box 10.

23. Davidson to Tate, 15 Feb. 1927; Tate to Davidson, 20 Feb. 1927, in *Correspondence of Davidson and Tate*, 185–90.

24. Donald Davidson, "The Artist as Southerner," *Saturday Review of Literature* 2 (15 May 1926): 781–83; Davidson, "Allen Tate: The Traditionalist as Modernist," in Davidson Papers, Box 17.

25. Tate to Davidson, 6 Feb. 1943, 11 Feb. 1943, Davidson Papers, Box 11.

26. Davidson to Kuhlman (letter draft), 1 March 1943, Davidson Papers, Box 1.

27. Purdy, *Fugitives' Reunion*; Tate to Davidson, 15 May 1956, Davidson Papers, Box 11.

28. Tate to Davidson, 23 Jan. 1962, 4 Feb. 1962, 27 April 1962, Davidson Papers, Box 11; Ransom to Tate, 16 April 1962, Ransom Papers (Young collection).

II. In Defense of the South

1. Davidson to Stark Young, 4 Aug. 1952, Davidson Papers, Box 2, SC.

2. Tate to Davidson, 8 July 1925, 2 Dec. 1925; Davidson to Tate, 29 Nov. 1925, in *Correspondence of Davidson and Tate*, 141–42, 150–54.

3. Edwin Mims, *The Advancing South: Stories of Progress and Reaction* (New York: Doubleday, Page, 1926); O'Brien, *American South*, 137–38.

4. Davidson, "First Fruits of Dayton, The Intellectual Evolution in Dixie," *Forum* 79 (June 1928): 896–907.

5. Davidson, *The Tall Men* (Boston: Houghton Mifflin, 1927); Davidson to a Mr. Linscott, 9 April 1927, Davidson Papers, Box 1.

6. Ransom to Tate, 18 June 1926, 5 September 1926; Ransom to Davidson, 5 September 1926, in *Letters of John Crowe Ransom*, 149–57.

7. Ransom to Robert Graves, 12 June 1925, 23 Sept. 1929, 2 Dec. 1925, ibid., 142–49.

8. Ransom to Tate, 5 Sept. 1926, [Spring] 1927, ibid., 154–57, 163–69.

9. Ransom to Tate, 3 and 13 April 1927, ibid., 169–74.

10. Tate to Davidson, 7 Sept. 1923, 14 April 1924, in Davidson Papers, Box 10.

11. Tate to Davidson, 11 July 1924, 25 Aug. 1924, 8 Dec. 1924, 17 Dec. 1924, 16 Jan. 1925, 16 Feb. 1925, 21 May 1925, ibid.

12. The best glimpses into the Tate family in these years is in *The Southern Mandarins: Letters of Caroline Gordon to Sally Wood, 1924–1937*, ed. Sally Wood (Baton Rouge: Louisiana State Univ. Press, 1984), 17–30.

13. Tate to Davidson, 3 March 1926, 26 June 1926, 29 July 1926, Davidson Papers, Box 10.

14. Tate to Davidson, 1 March 1927, in *Correspondence of Davidson and Tate*, 191–92.

15. Davidson to Tate, 4 March 1927, 21 March 1927; Tate to Davidson, 17 March 1927, ibid., 191–92, 195–96; Ransom to Tate, 3 and 13 April 1927, *Letters of John Crowe Ransom*, 169–74.

16. Tate, *Stonewall Jackson, The Good Soldier* (New York: Balch, 1928).

17. John C. Ransom, "The South—Old or New," *Sewanee Review* 36 (April 1928): 139–47.

18. Ransom to Tate, [Fall] 1927, Ransom Papers (Young collection).

19. Wood, *Mandarins*, 40–49.

20. Tate, *Jefferson Davis: His Rise and Fall* (New York: Minton, Balch & Co., 1929) passim, but p. 255 for the quotation.

21. Tate, "Humanism and Naturalism," in Tate, *Poetry and Ideas* (New York: Scribners, 1936), 113–44.

22. Ransom to Tate, 4 July 1929, in *Letters of John Crowe Ransom*, 179–83.

23. Ransom, *God Without Thunder: An Unorthodox Defense of Orthodoxy* (New York: Harcourt, Brace, 1930), passim.

24. Davidson to Tate, 5 Feb. 1929, in *Correspondence of Davidson and Tate*, 218–22.

25. Davidson to Tate, 29 July 1929, ibid,. 226–29.

26. Tate to Davidson, 10 Aug. 1929, ibid., 229–33.

III. The Book

1. Fletcher to Davidson, 26 June 1927, 24 Oct. 1927, 28 Feb. 1930, 12 April 1930, 16 May 1930, 25 June 1930, 10 Aug. 1930, 11 April 1933, in Davidson Papers, Box 5, SC.

2. Warren To Davidson, 8 July 1925, 21 Aug. 1925, 16 Feb. 1930, 25 June 1930, in Davidson Papers, Box 12.

3. Purdy, *Fugitives' Reunion,* 208-10.

4. Lytle to Davidson, 1 Feb. 1927, 21 Feb. 1929, in Davidson Papers, Box 7; Mark Lucas, *The Southern Vision of Andrew Lytle* (Baton Rouge: Louisiana State Univ. Press, 1986), 4-7.

5. Biographical details on Owsley, prepared by his wife, are in Box 6, Papers of Frank Owsley, SC.

6. O'Brien, *American South,* 97-113.

7. Kline to Davidson, 21 May 1930, 2 June 1930, 27 Sept. 1930, in Davidson Papers, Box 6.

8. Sarah Newman Shouse, *Hillbilly Realist: Herman Clarence Nixon of Possum Trot* (University, Ala: Univ. of Alabama Press, 1986), 5-42.

9. Young to Davidson, 4 June 1929, 25 June 1930, 1 July 1930, in Davidson Papers, Box 12.

10. Davidson to authors of *I'll Take My Stand,* 3 January 1941, Davidson Papers, Box 2.

11. Tate to E. F. Saxon, 3 Sept. 1930, in Davidson Papers, Box 1; Tate to Davidson, 24 July 1930, Davidson Papers, Box 10; Tate to Davidson, 3 Sept. 1930, 7 Sept. 1930, Davidson to Tate, 5 Sept. 1930, in *Correspondence of Davidson and Tate,* 252-55.

12. Davidson to Warren, 17 March 1930, Davidson Papers, Box 1; Davidson to Tate, 21 July 1930, in *Correspondence of Davidson and Tate,* 250-52.

13. Tate to Davidson, 22 July 1930, Davidson Papers, Box 10.

14. Tate to Davidson, 10 Aug. 1929; Davidson to Tate, 29 Dec. 1929, in *Correspondence of Davidson and Tate,* 229-32, 246-49; Ransom to Tate, 5 Jan. 1930; Ransom to Warren, 20 Jan. 1930; Ransom to Tate, 15 March 1930, in *Letters of John Crowe Ransom,* 188-93, 196-99.

15. "Articles of Agrarian Reform," Davidson Papers, Box 17.

16. Ransom to Tate, 15 Feb. 1930, Ransom Papers (Young collection), SC.

17. Twelve Southerners, *I'll Take My Stand; The South and the Agrarian Tradition* (New York: Harper, 1930; repr. New York: Harper Torch Books, 1962), ix-xxiv.

18. Ibid., xxiv-xxviii.

19. Ibid., xxviii-xxx.

20. Ibid., passim.

21. Ibid., 3–27.

22. Ibid., 94–96, 110–11, 114–21.

23. Ibid., 28–60.

24. Ibid., x, 249–64; Rubin, 335–36.

25. Singal, *The War Within,* 348–49.

26. O'Brien, *American South,* 163–68; Twelve Southerners, *Stand,* 69–91; Purdy, *Fugitives' Reunion,* 203–205.

27. Tate to Ransom, 27 July 1929, in Davidson Papers, Box 10.

28. O'Brien, *American South,* 146–49; Twelve Southerners, *Stand,* 155–66.

29. Twelve Southerners, *Stand,* 166–75.

30. Ibid., 122–54.

31. Ibid., 201–45.

32. Ibid., 176–200.

33. Ibid.

34. The collection of reviews is in Davidson Papers, Box 35.

35. William C. Havard and Walter Sullivan, eds., *A Band of Prophets: The Vanderbilt Agrarians After Fifty Years* (Baton Rouge: Louisiana State Univ. Press, 1982), 8–9, 15–16.

IV. The Movement

1. Warren to Tate, 6 Sept. 1930, in Davidson Papers, Box 12, SC; clippings on the debate are in Davidson Papers, Box 35.

2. Tate to Davidson, 3 Sept. 1930, Davidson Papers, Box 10; Owsley to Davidson, 8 April 1931, Davidson Papers, Box 8; minutes of a 22 Nov. 1931 meeting of Agrarians, to form an Agrarian Party, in Davidson Papers, Box 19.

3. Davidson to Tate, 13 Dec. 1930, Davidson Papers, Box 10.

4. Davidson to Tate, 29 Oct. 1932, in *Correspondence of Davidson and Tate,* 271–79.

5. Wood, *Mandarins,* 68–94, 209; Robert Lowell, "Meeting the Tates," *Sewanee Review* 67 (Fall 1959): 557–59.

6. Wood, *Mandarins,* 68–94.

7. Tate to Davidson, 10 Dec. 1931, Davidson Papers, Box 10.

8. Davidson to Tate, 29 Oct. 1932, *Correspondence of Davidson and Tate,* 271–79.

9. Tate to Davidson, 10 Dec. 1932, ibid., 279–80.

10. This famous essay first appeared in two volumes of *American*

Review 2 (Nov. and Dec. 1933): 58–72, 175–88; see also "The Sacred Harp in the Land of Eden," *Virginia Quarterly Review* 10 (April 1934): 203–17.

11. Davidson, "Howard Odum and the Sociological Proteus," a review of *Southern Regions of the United States,* in *American Review* 7 (Feb. 1937): 385–417; "Where Regionalism and Sectionalism Meet," *Social Forces* 13 (Oct. 1934): 23–31.

12. Ibid.; Davidson, "Regionalism as Social Science," *Southern Review* 3 (Oct. 1937): 209–24. Davidson's best essays on regionalism are collected in *The Attack on Leviathan, Regionalism and Nationalism in the United States* (Chapel Hill: Univ. of North Carolina Press, 1938).

13. Ransom to Tate, 19 May 1932, and 29 Oct. 1932, in *Letters of John Crowe Ransom,* 207–11.

14. Ransom, "Land! An Answer to the Unemployment Problem," *Harper's Magazine* 165 (July 1932): 216–24; Ransom, "Happy Farmers," *American Review* 1 (Oct. 1933): 513–35.

15. This "Memorandum" is in Davidson Papers, Box 19.

16. Tate to Davidson, 23 Feb. 1936, Davidson Papers, Box 10.

17. Tate to Eugene F. Saxon, 17 Nov. 1933, in Davidson Papers, Box 10.

18. Owsley to Fletcher, Dec. 1933, and 11 March 1934, Owsley Papers, Box 6, SC; Davidson to Fletcher, 26 March 1934, Davidson Papers, Box 1.

19. Hilaire Belloc, "The Restoration of Property," *American Review* 1 (April, May, June, Sept., Oct. 1933): 204–19, 257–85, 344–57, 468–82, 600–609; and 2 (Nov. 1933): 46–57.

20. Tate, "Notes on Liberty and Property," *American Review* 6 (March 1936): 596–611; Ransom, "What Does the South Want?" in *Who Owns America? A New Declaration of Independence,* ed. Herbert Agar and Allen Tate (Boston: Houghton Mifflin, 1936), 178–93.

21. Frank Owsley, "The Pillars of Agrarianism," *American Review* 4 (March 1935): 529–47.

22. Davidson, "Where are the Laymen, A Study in Policy Making," *American Review* 9 (Oct. 1937): 456–81; Shouse, *Hillbilly Realist,* 78–89; Tate to Davidson, 11 May 1936, Davidson Papers, Box 10.

23. Davidson, "I'll Take My Stand: A History," *American Review* 5 (Summer 1935): 301–21.

24. Davis to Davidson, 17 Jan. 1934, 14 Sept. 1934, 28 Feb. 1935, in Davidson Papers, Box 4; Fletcher to Davidson, 5 March, 11 March, 12

March (telegram), 13 March, 25 March, 25 April, 18 May 1935, Davidson Papers, Box 5.

25. Davidson to Fletcher, 23 Jan. 1950, Davidson Papers, Box 5; Charlie May Fletcher to Davidson, 17 May 1950, 17 Sept. 1950, Davidson Papers, Box 5.

26. Wood, *Mandarins,* 191–94; Owsley to Tate, 12 Nov. 1935, Owsley Papers, Box 6; Tate to Davidson, 4 Dec. 1942, Davidson Papers, Box 11.

27. Nixon to Owsley, 25 Oct. 1935, Owsley Papers, Box 4.

28. Agar and Tate, *Who Owns America?,* 18–35, 52–67, 80–93, 113–34, 237–79.

29. Ibid., 178–93.

30. Letter to the members of the Nashville conference, 31 August 1936, Andrew Lytle Papers, Box 9, SC.

31. Minutes of convention held by the Committee for the Alliance of Agrarian and Distributist Groups, Nashville, 4–5 June 1936, ibid.

32. Ransom to Tate, 3 Dec. 1936, Ransom Papers (Young collection); Ransom to Baker Brownell, 29 Jan. 1937, Ransom Papers (Young collection).

V. In Retreat

1. Tate to Davidson, 4 Dec. 1942, Davidson Papers, Box 11, SC.

2. Ransom to Tate, 17 Dec. 1936, 11 March and 6 April 1937, Ransom Papers (Young collection), SC; Ransom, "Art and the Human Economy," *Kenyon Review* 7 (Autumn 1945): 683–88.

3. Ransom, "Art and the Human Economy."

4. Paul K. Conkin, *Gone with the Ivy: A Biography of Vanderbilt University* (Knoxville: Univ. of Tennessee Press, 1985), 391–98.

5. Ibid., 398–400.

6. Ransom to Tate, 19 Oct. 1937, and 1 Jan. 1938, Ransom Papers (Young collection).

7. Ransom to Tate, 1 Jan. 1938, 23 May 1941, in *Letters of John Crowe Ransom,* 235–37, 282–83.

8. Tate, "The Present Function of Criticism," in *Collected Essays* (Denver: Alan Swallow, 1959), 3–15; Tate, "Literature as Knowledge," ibid., 16–48.

9. Tate, "Understanding Modern Poetry," ibid., 115–28; Tate, "Tension in Poetry," ibid., 75–90.

10. Ransom, "Criticism, Inc.," in *Selected Essays of John Crowe Ransom*, ed. Thomas Daniel Young and John Hindle (Baton Rouge: Louisiana State Univ. Press, 1984), 93–106; Ransom, "The Literary Criticism of Aristotle," ibid., 232–48.

11. Ransom, "Wanted: An Ontologic Critic," ibid., 147–79.

12. Ransom, "Criticism as Pure Speculation," ibid., 128–46.

13. Cleanth Brooks, Jr., and Robert Penn Warren, *Understanding Poetry: An Anthology for College Students* (New York: Holt, 1938).

14. These views are clearest in a series of lectures published as *Southern Writers in the Modern World* (Athens: Univ. of Georgia Press, 1958).

15. Owsley, *Plain Folk of the Old South* (Baton Rouge: Louisiana State Univ. Press, 1949).

16. Owsley to Tate, 29 Feb. 1932, 26 May 1937, Owsley Papers, Box 6, SC.

17. Owsley to Tate, 20 April 1941, 30 April 1931, ibid.; Owsley to Warren, 24 January 1950, ibid.

18. Owsley to a Mr. Stone, 24 May 1938, ibid.; Owsley to Tate, 14 Nov. 1943, 13 Aug. 1944, ibid.; Owsley to Herschel Gower, 4 Nov. 1955, ibid.

19. Owsley to Tate, 12 Nov. 1935, 14 Dec. 1955, ibid.; Owsley to Warren, 25 August 1946, ibid.; Owsley to a Mr. Carter, 14 March 1952, ibid.; Purdy, *Fugitives' Reunion*, 204–205.

20. Lytle to Owsley, 23 March 1939, 6 Jan. 1948, 26 Feb. 1956, Owsley Papers, Box 3.

21. Davidson, "The Class Approach to Southern Problems," *Southern Review* 5 (Autumn 1939): 261–72; Davidson, "Agrarianism and Politics," *Review of Politics* 1 (April 1939): 114–25.

22. Davidson, "The Mystery of the Agrarians," *Saturday Review* 26 (23 Jan. 1943), 6–7

23. Owsley, "Scottsboro, The Third Crusade; The Sequel to Abolition and Reconstruction," *American Review* 1 (June 1933): 257–85; Davidson to Fletcher, 7 April 1933, Davidson Papers, Box 1.

24. Davidson to Wade, 3 March 1934, Davidson Papers, Box 1.

25. Davidson, "The Sacred Harp in the Land of Eden," *Virginia Quarterly Review* 10 (April 1934): 203–17; Davidson, "The Trend of Southern Letters," unpublished manuscript, Davidson Papers, Box 21.

26. Davidson, "Preface to Decision," *Sewanee Review* 53 (Summer 1945): 394–412.

27. Davidson, "The New South and the Conservative Tradition," *National Review* 9 (10 Sept. 1960): 141–46; Wade to Davidson, 8 Aug. 1954, 24 Dec. 1955, Davidson Papers, Box 11.

28. Ransom to Tate, 29 Aug. 1942, Ransom Papers (Young collection).

29. Davidson to Tate, 31 March 1937, in *Correspondence of Davidson and Tate,* 300–302.

30. Davidson to Tate, 2 Jan. 1943, 3 Oct. 1945, ibid., 329–32, 344–45; Davidson to Owsley, 5 Feb. 1950, Owsley Papers, Box 2.

31. Davidson to Randall Stewart, 22 Feb. 1955, Davidson Papers, Box 2.

32. Davidson to Tate, 26 Jan. 1951, *Correspondence of Davidson and Tate,* 353–54.

33. Davidson to Tate, 4 May 1952, ibid., 364–65; Tate to Davidson, 19 Oct. 1962, 23 Nov. 1963, Davidson Papers, Box 11.

34. This speech is in the Fugitive-Agrarian Collection, Box 2, SC.

35. The uncompleted novel is in SC.

Index